Close-up

WORKBOOK

B1

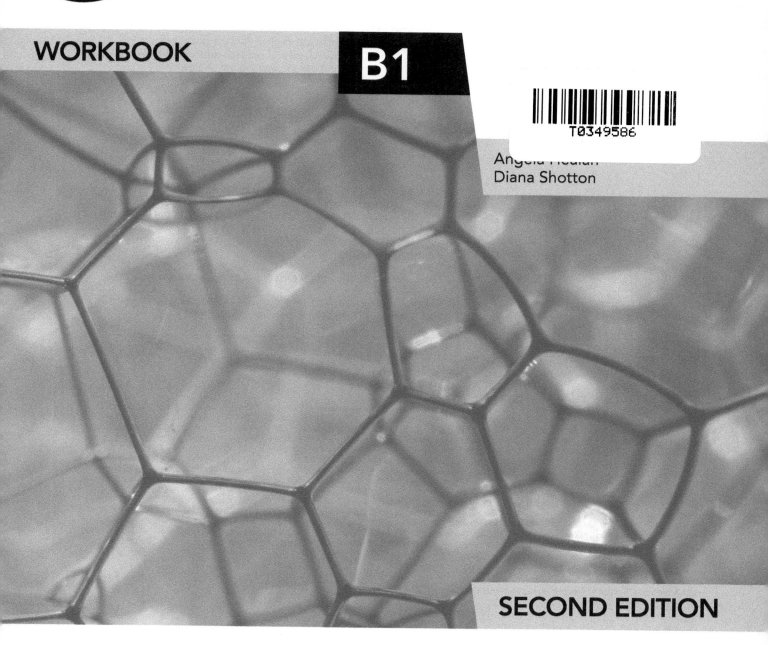

Angela Healan
Diana Shotton

SECOND EDITION

NATIONAL GEOGRAPHIC
LEARNING

Australia · Brazil · Mexico · Singapore · United Kingdom · United States

NATIONAL GEOGRAPHIC
L E A R N I N G

Close-up B1 Workbook, Second Edition

Angela Healan
Diana Shotton

Publisher: Sharon Jervis

Development Editor: Kayleigh Buller

Editorial Assistant: Georgina McComb

Text/Cover Designer: Ken Vail Graphic Design

Content Project Manager: Jon Ricketts

Editorial Liaison: Leila Hishmeh

For product information and technology assistance, contact us at
Cengage Learning Customer & Sales Support, cengage.com/contact

For permission to use material from this text or product, submit all requests online at **cengage.com/permissions**
Further permissions questions can be emailed to
permissionrequest@cengage.com

ISBN: 978-1-4080-9556-0

National Geographic Learning
Cheriton House, North Way, Andover, Hampshire, SP10 5BE
United Kingdom

National Geographic Learning, a Cengage Learning Company, has a mission to bring the world to the classroom and the classroom to life. With our English language programs, students learn about their world by experiencing it. Through our partnerships with National Geographic and TED Talks, they develop the language and skills they need to be successful global citizens and leaders.

Locate your local office at **international.cengage.com/region**

Visit National Geographic Learning online at **NGL.Cengage.com/ELT**
Visit our corporate website at **www.cengage.com**

Photo credits

Cover image: (front cover) © Charles Krebs/Corbis, (back cover) nikkytok/Shutterstock

Shutterstock:

3 Frantisekhojdysz; **3** Greg Epperson; **4** Nikkytok; **4** Katie Smith Photography; **5** Wavebreakmedia; **6** Atlaspix; **7** Monkey Business Images; **8** Shutterstock; **9** Nikkytok; **9** Mircea Bezergheanu; **10** MNStudio; **11** Creatista; **12** Joao Virissimo; **12** Rohit Seth; **13** Shutterstock; **14** Odua Images; **15** Edyta Pawlowska; **16** Nikkytok; **16** Topseller; **17** LysFoto; **18** Nikkytok; **18** Footage.Pro; **19** Incredible Arctic; **20** Shutterstock; **21** Catalin Petolea; **21** Celso Diniz; **21** Irina Bondareva; **21** David Maska; **22** Angela Hawkey; **24** Wikus Otto; **25** Shutterstock; **26** Odua Images; **27** Edyta Pawlowska; **28** Nikkytok; **29** Stephen Coburn; **30** Markabond; **31** Hannamariah; **32** Shutterstock; **33** Nikkytok; **34** Elena Elisseeva; **35** Kungvery lucky; **35** Photographee.eu; **35** Africa Studio; **35** Davor Ratkovic; **35** Davor Ratkovic; **35** Davor Ratkovic; **35** Davor Ratkovic; **35** Davor Ratkovic; **35** Renata Novackova; **35** Renata Novackova; **35** Renata Novackova; **35** Wiktoria Pawlak; **35** Wiktoria Pawlak; **35** Wiktoria Pawlak; **35** Krylovochka; **35** Miguel Angel Salinas Salinas; **35** Krylovochka; **35** Ollyy; **36** Christos Georghiou; **37** Shutterstock; **37** Sebastian Duda; **38** Odua Images; **39** Edyta Pawlowska; **40** Vlue; **40** Nikkytok; **40** Mikenorton; **41** Monkey Business Images; **42** Stefan Pircher; **43** Emin Kuliyev; **44** Shutterstock; **44** Ludmila Yilmaz; **45** Nikkytok; **45** Shutterstock; **45** Darko Zeljkovic; **46** Lucky Business; **47** Ivica Drusany; **48** Shutterstock; **48** Lisa F. Young; **49** Shutterstock; **49** CandyBox Images; **50** Odua Images; **51** Edyta Pawlowska; **52** Nikkytok; **52** Monkey Business Images; **53** Nesa Cera; **54** Alan Ward; **55** Szasz-Fabian Jozsef; **56** Shutterstock; **56** Violetkaipa; **57** Nikkytok; **58** Bubica; **58** Bubica; **59** Air Images; **60** Holbox; **61** Shutterstock; **62** Odua Images; **63** Edyta Pawlowska; **64** Nikkytok; **65** Loraks; **66** Mamahoohooba; **67** Ustyujanin; **68** Shutterstock; **69** Nikkytok; **69** Maxfx; **69** Shutterstock; **71** Milosz_G; **71** Sunabesyou; **71** Maxene Huiyu; **71** Rui Vale Sousa; **71** Marvi7; **71** Veronchick84; **71** Kiss Beetle; **71** Elenapro; **71** Hobitnjak; **71** Gleb Stock; **71** Rui Vale Sousa; **71** Elenapro; **71** Cube29; **71** Excess; **72** Lukiyanova Natalia/frenta; **72** Inga Lvanova; **73** Shutterstock; **74** Odua Images; **75** Edyta Pawlowska.

1 Charles Krebs/Corbis; **16** Nobert Rosing/National Geographic.

Illustrations: Illustrations by Panagiotis Angeletakis

The publisher has made every effort to trace and contact copyright holders before publication. If any have been inadvertently overlooked, the publisher will be pleased to rectify any errors or omissions at the earliest opportunity.

Printed in the United Kingdom by Ashford Colour Ltd.
Print Number: 16   Print Year: 2025

Reading

A Read the *Exam Reminder*. Which words should you <u>underline</u>?

_____

B Now complete the *Exam Task*.

Twins

Have you ever wondered what it would be like to have a brother or a sister who looked just like you? Maybe you *are* a twin. Holly and Daisy Preston, 14-year-old twins from London, say there's nothing like it. 'I feel really special,' says Holly. Daisy agrees and adds, 'It's fantastic having someone who understands you completely.' If you are a twin, you probably know what they are talking about!

Scientists think twins are great, too, but for different reasons. They give scientists a unique opportunity to find out what makes us who we are. That's because twins have more in common than brothers and sisters born at different times, but are still different from each other in important ways. By studying the similarities and differences between twins, scientists can begin to find out which qualities are passed down from our ancestors and which ones result from our experiences in life.

There are two kinds of twins, known as identical and fraternal. Identical twins are often so similar that it is difficult to tell them apart. Twins that grow inside their mother at the same time, but are not identical, are called fraternal twins. These twins can be both boys, both girls, or one of each.

Identical twins are interesting to scientists because of their genes, which determine the colour of their hair and eyes, the shape of their nose and mouth, their height and more. Most people get a different mixture of genes from their parents. That explains why you might take after your mother, while your sister takes after your father. But with identical twins, each one gets passed down exactly the same genes from each parent. That is what makes them 'identical'.

Exam Reminder

Reading the exam question first

- Before you read the text, remember to read the exam statements carefully.
- Make sure you underline key words in each statement so you know what information to look for.
- Read the text quickly so you know what it is about. Then read the text again and look for words that are similar to the words you underlined.
- Remember that the information in the text is in the same order as the statements.

Scientists have always wondered how important genes are. Yes, they determine which relative we look like, but what about personality? Do our genes control whether we like music or are outgoing? Or, are our personalities a result of the way we grow up and the experiences we have? Interestingly, researchers have discovered that both our genes and our experiences play a role in forming our personality. For example, you may have a gene that makes you creative, but if your environment does not give you the chance to show your creativity, it may never be revealed.

Identical twins can show us this relationship between genes and environment. If it were only our genes that influenced everything about us, identical twins would be identical in every way. Not only would they look the same, but they would like the same kinds of music, clothes and friends. But they don't. Studying such differences can help scientists to find out what makes us the same and what makes us different.

Exam Task

Look at the sentences below about twins. Read the text to decide if each sentence is correct or incorrect. Write **T** (True) or **F** (False).

1 Holly and Daisy are sisters. ☐
2 Holly and Daisy understand each other well. ☐
3 Scientists think twins are great because being a twin is a unique opportunity. ☐
4 It is always easy to tell identical twins apart. ☐
5 Fraternal twins look the same. ☐
6 Genes do not control our eye colour. ☐

7 Identical twins get the same genes from their mother and father. ☐
8 Genes control who we look like. ☐
9 Scientists learned that personality depends on genes and environment. ☐
10 Identical twins like the same music. ☐

Vocabulary

A Complete the sentences with these words.

aunt   cousins   grandmother   nephew   niece   step-mother

1 Your _____ is the sister of your mother or father.
2 Your _____ are the children of your uncle or aunt.
3 Your _____ is the mother of your mother or father.
4 Your _____ is the wife of your father if he marries someone who isn't your mother.
5 Your _____ is the son of your sister or brother.
6 Your _____ is the daughter of your sister or brother.

B Complete the words in the sentences.

1 My e _ _ _ _ _ _ grandparents live with us because they are too old to look after themselves.
2 Don't worry. If Carrie says she'll help you, she will. She's very r _ _ _ _ _ _ _, you know.
3 Fred is quite l _ _ _. He never helps me with the cooking and cleaning.
4 You can't wear jeans to your sister's wedding, Barry! You'll look really s _ _ _ _ _ _!
5 Vera wanted an h _ _ _ _ _ opinion about her wedding dress, so I told her the truth.
6 How can my parents understand me? They're not young any more – they're m _ _ _ _ _ - _ _ _ _!

Grammar

Present Simple & Present Continuous

A Circle the correct words.

1 Angela is living / lives in Paris. She was born there and never left.
2 Mum, where are you? Quick! The dinner is burning / burns!
3 Russ and Katy are planning / plan their wedding next year.
4 Dad usually does / does usually the supermarket shopping after work.
5 It gets / It's getting harder and harder to have a family in the city.
6 Genes determine / are determining your hair and eye colour.
7 My brother and sister are always arguing / are arguing always. It really annoys me!
8 Brian, what do you do / are you doing this weekend? Do you want to go fishing?
9 The Greeks and the Italians have / are having very large families.
10 The train to my mum's village leaves / is leaving at nine o'clock every morning.

B Tick (✓) if the sentence is correct. Rewrite the incorrect sentences.

1 I am knowing Jim very well because we went to university together. _____
2 We don't often visit our cousins in the countryside. _____
3 My grandfather is a scientist and he is liking to invent things. _____
4 Michael is a chef, but never he cooks at home for his family! _____
5 Teenagers become more and more independent these days. _____
6 The sun is rising in the east and it is setting in the west. _____
7 Why does your little sister cry? Is she thirsty? _____
8 Tim wants to buy a house, but Helen thinks they should wait until next year. _____

Listening

A Read the *Exam Reminder*. Why should you look at each set of pictures?

_____

B 1.1 ▶️ Listen and complete the *Exam Task*.

Exam Reminder

Identifying differences

- Remember to read the question and underline any key words for each set of pictures before you listen.
- Then look at the pictures and check you understand them. Identify the differences between the pictures before listening.

Exam Task

There are six questions in this part. For each question, there are three pictures and a short recording. Circle the correct picture **a**, **b** or **c**.

1 Which photo are they looking at?

2 What do the girls look like?

3 Where do the cousins buy their clothes?

4 What does her brother like to do with friends?

5 Which day were they going to go shopping?

6 Which is her son?

C 1.1 ▶️ Listen again and check your answers.

Vocabulary

A Complete the text with these words in the correct form. You can use some of them more than once.

> fall get have keep pay

Summer love

When Joe returned from his holiday in Spain, he brought back more than a few souvenirs. He had some very exciting news. He was going to (**1**) _____ married! His family and friends couldn't believe it. Who? When? How? They had so many questions! 'Well,' explained Joe, 'I met Carmen in Barcelona and we (**2**) _____ in love.' Joe didn't want to (**3**) _____ any secrets from his family, so he told them everything. 'She worked at the hotel where I was staying. She's very pretty, so I (**4**) _____ her a compliment and asked her out for a coffee. Before I knew it, we were spending all our time together.' 'When can we meet her?' asked his mother. 'Soon,' replied Joe. 'She's going to (**5**) _____ us a visit next month.' His mother was worried. 'But you hardly know her. You don't want to make a mistake and then (**6**) _____ divorced in a couple of years!' she said. 'Don't worry, Mum,' replied Joe. 'Everything will be fine.' And Joe was right. Twenty years later, Joe and Carmen now (**7**) _____ a family and are still living happily ever after!

B Circle the correct words.

1 Sam's father left his mother. Sam's worried that she'll fall to pieces / in love.

2 I have a lot of sympathy / families for children of divorced parents.

3 My grandmother's house is near here; let's go and pay her a compliment / a visit.

4 A lot of my friends keep a diary / a secret; they write in it every day.

5 My sister is getting married / divorced at the end of the month – she's having a traditional wedding.

6 Do you plan to have sympathy / a family when you grow up? I want a big one with five children!

Grammar

Countable / Uncountable Nouns & Quantifiers

A Complete the text with these words.

> a lot   few   little   lot of   many   much   number   some

She's the boss!

The Mosuo people live in China and they are one of only a **(1)** _____ matriarchal societies in the world. In a matriarchal society, the head of the family is the mother. The family name passes down from female to female, and the women make all the decisions.

(2) _____ generations of women – great-grandmothers, grandmothers, mothers and daughters – live in the same house with a **(3)** _____ their male relatives, such as uncles, brothers, sons and nephews. Fathers or husbands live elsewhere and they only have a **(4)** _____ contact with their children.

The children belong to the mother and her family. The uncles help with the children's education and care, but they don't have **(5)** _____ control. In time, the children care for their elderly uncles. These large extended families care **(6)** _____ about each other.

The modern world, however, is affecting **(7)** _____ traditions and things are changing very quickly. Many young people leave their villages to work in a **(8)** _____ of large cities nearby. There, they may discover a different way of life and a culture that is very different to their own.

B Complete the sentences with the correct Present Simple form of the verb *be*.

1 Where _____ the information I am looking for?
2 There _____ many people in my family tree.
3 That _____ great advice. Thanks, Dad!
4 Maths _____ my favourite subject at school.
5 My mirror _____ broken. I need a new one.
6 Their traditions _____ quite strange, I think.
7 The food _____ cold. Can you put it back in the oven, please?
8 This family research _____ very important.

Use your English

A Choose the correct answers.

Who do you think you are?

Genealogy is hugely popular because people are curious to know about their ancestors. There are even TV programmes about genealogy. The most well-known one **(1)** _____ a series called *Who Do You Think You Are?* In each episode, genealogists **(2)** _____ a celebrity to trace his or her family tree. They use the Internet and paper records to discover the past. Sometimes, the records go back hundreds of years and people discover that their **(3)** _____ were kings, queens, or something more normal, such as farmers, cowboys or soldiers.

If your past interests you, it isn't difficult to find **(4)** _____ of this information on the Internet. **(5)** _____ official records are available online. The more information you discover, the more interested you become. It's hard to stop looking! **(6)** _____ people are **(7)** _____ their past, and maybe you can, too.

1	a	are	b	is	c	has
2	a	help	b	helps	c	is helping
3	a	members	b	families	c	relatives
4	a	few	b	some	c	lot
5	a	Many	b	Much	c	A little
6	a	A lot of	b	A lot	c	Lot of
7	a	discover	b	discovering	c	discovers

writing: an email

A Match the abbreviations to their meanings.

1	e.g.	☐	**a**	twentieth
2	am	☐	**b**	street
3	i.e.	☐	**c**	the United Kingdom
4	USA	☐	**d**	for example
5	St	☐	**e**	that's to say
6	UK	☐	**f**	morning
7	pm	☐	**g**	afternoon
8	20th	☐	**h**	the United States of America

Learning Reminder

Using abbreviations
Remember to use these common abbreviations in postcards and notes:
- *am* (morning) and *pm* (afternoon)
- titles for people, e.g. *Mrs*, *Miss*, *Ms*, *Mr* and *Dr*
- parts of the language, e.g. *etc.* (etcetera), *e.g.* (for example) and *i.e.* (that's to say)
- ordinal numbers, e.g. *1st* (first) and *20th* (twentieth)
- addresses, e.g. *St* (street), *Ave* (avenue) and *Rd* (road)
- some countries, e.g. *USA* (the United States of America), *UAE* (the United Arab Emirates) and *UK* (the United Kingdom)

B Read the writing task below and then circle the correct answer, *a* or *b*.

You are planning a party for your grandparents' 50th wedding anniversary. Write an email to one of your relatives inviting him or her to the party.

In your invitation you should:
- *say what the invitation is for*
- *say when the party is*
- *say who is coming*

1 a You are having a party for your grandfather's 50th birthday.
  b You are celebrating your grandparents' 50 years of marriage.

2 a You must write a formal email.
  b You must write an informal email.

3 a You will send the email to a member of your family.
  b You will send the email to someone you don't know.

C Read the example email and <u>underline</u> the abbreviations.

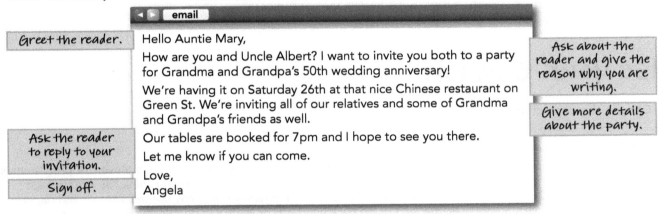

Greet the reader.

> **email**
>
> Hello Auntie Mary,
>
> How are you and Uncle Albert? I want to invite you both to a party for Grandma and Grandpa's 50th wedding anniversary!
>
> We're having it on Saturday 26th at that nice Chinese restaurant on Green St. We're inviting all of our relatives and some of Grandma and Grandpa's friends as well.
>
> Our tables are booked for 7pm and I hope to see you there.
>
> Let me know if you can come.
>
> Love,
> Angela

Ask about the reader and give the reason why you are writing.

Give more details about the party.

Ask the reader to reply to your invitation.

Sign off.

D Read and complete the *Exam Task* below. Don't forget to use the *Useful Expressions* on page 15 of your Student's Book.

Exam Task

Your older brother has got into a good university and your parents want to have a surprise party for him. Write an email to one of his friends inviting him or her to the party.

In your email you should:

- tell his friend why you are emailing
- give information about the party (time, place, date)
- ask his friend to reply (35–45 words)

▶ Writing Reference p. 176 in Student's Book

Reading

A Read the *Exam Reminder*. Should you read the text or the answer options first?

_____

B Now complete the *Exam Task*.

Honey

Honey is a natural sweetener with nothing artificial added. Many people believe it's (**1**) _____ for you than sugar. It's easy to eat, you can use it in a variety of recipes and it lasts for a very long time. Although most people think of honey as no more than a sweetener for tea or yoghurt, honey has many health benefits, too.

Imagine this: you can't sleep because your nose is blocked and you can't stop coughing. Colds make us feel miserable and coughing stops us from sleeping, so (**2**) _____ of people take pills and cough syrups to get better. Scientific research, however, has shown that there's no evidence that these medicines work. (**3**) _____ doctors are now suggesting that we take honey to help (**4**) _____ improve our health. It has been harvested and used as a medicine for hundreds of years by civilisations all over the world. How does honey help? Well, because it's a thick and sticky liquid, it coats the inside of your throat and can stop you coughing. It also contains substances that are very important to help prevent diseases. These substances are known as antioxidants and are also found in fresh fruit and vegetables, olive oil and oregano.

Honey is also great for athletes and anyone who needs extra energy. The human body gets most of

(**5**) _____ energy from carbohydrates (natural sugars). Foods such as bread, rice, pasta and potatoes have plenty of carbohydrates. Honey also contains a lot of them. Carbohydrates are necessary for athletes to (**6**) _____ them keep going when they are training, so it's a good idea to eat honey before exercising, or (**7**) _____ sport.

There are lots (**8**) _____ healthy ways to enjoy honey. Try mixing it with yoghurt, fruit and crushed nuts, or you can make a tasty honey sandwich. You can even make your own energy bars filled (**9**) _____ dried fruit, cereal and honey. Whether you need an energy boost, or just something deliciously sweet to eat, honey is the perfect natural energy source.

But that's not all! You (**10**) _____ use honey to make your own fantastic beauty products. Mix strawberries, honey, almond oil and a drop of vitamin E oil to make a natural lip gloss. Or, make a conditioner for your hair from honey and olive oil. Look for beauty recipes online. It's usually a simple process, they cost you almost nothing to make, and they're all natural.

Honey – so good in so many ways.

Exam Task

Read the text and choose the correct word for each space. For each question, mark the correct letter **a**, **b**, **c** or **d**.

#	a		b		c		d	
1	a	good	b	better	c	well	d	best
2	a	many	b	lot	c	lots	d	several
3	a	Some	b	None	c	Someone	d	Everyone
4	a	me	b	us	c	you	d	them
5	a	our	b	his	c	my	d	its
6	a	give	b	help	c	stop	d	save
7	a	playing	b	making	c	going	d	having
8	a	for	b	at	c	of	d	on
9	a	on	b	of	c	in	d	with
10	a	can	b	do	c	will	d	can't

Vocabulary

A Choose the correct answers.

| delicious | horrible | hungry | thirsty |

1 Could I have a glass of water, please? I'm extremely _____.

| bowl | dessert | knife | starter |

2 I think I'll have the chicken for my _____. What about you?

| frying | chewing | grilling | boiling |

3 Would you mind _____ the water so we can cook the eggs, please?

| breakfast | dessert | kitchen | starter |

4 Ben and Jerry always have ice cream for _____.

| chop | cook | mix | peel |

5 You have to _____ a banana before you can eat it!

| boil | fry | grill | stir |

6 Put the ingredients into a bowl and _____ with a spoon.

B Complete the words in the sentences.

1 W_ _ _ _ is a very useful grain.

2 You need e_ _ _ and flour to make cakes.

3 My least favourite green vegetable is b_ _ _ _ _ _ _.

4 I love cheese and tomatoes, so p_ _ _ _ is my favourite food.

5 We usually eat c_ _ _ _ _ _ _ _ for breakfast at the weekend.

Grammar

Past Simple; Past Continuous

A Circle the correct words.

1 Sam took a shower, had breakfast and left / was leaving for school.

2 I was sure I knew / was knowing the answer to the question.

3 Glen was chopping broccoli when he dropped / was dropping a knife.

4 Frank had / was having a coffee with his friends last Sunday morning.

5 We bought / were buying a new fridge last month.

6 Peter was cooking the rice while Andrew fried / was frying the chicken.

7 The waiters were rushing around and the diners ate / were eating when I arrived at the restaurant.

8 When you phoned me last night, I watched / was watching *MasterChef*.

B Complete the sentences with the Past Simple or the Past Continuous form of the verbs in brackets.

1 The customers _____ (hate) the food, so the restaurant _____ (close).

2 The chef _____ (watch) TV so he _____ (forget) about the food.

3 While the waiter _____ (talk) to Mrs Green, he _____ (drop) the food on her.

4 First, I _____ (fry) the fish and then I _____ (boil) the eggs.

5 Don't worry. We _____ (not have) dinner when you _____ (call).

6 I _____ (order) a dessert after my spaghetti, but I _____ (be) too full to eat it.

7 Veronica _____ (read) a cookbook while her children _____ (play) in the garden.

8 Fred _____ (not go) to the restaurant because he _____ (not feel) well.

Listening

A Read the *Exam Reminder*. Why should you be careful with numbers and dates?

_____

B `2.1` ▷ Listen and complete the *Exam Task*.

Exam Task

You will hear part of a radio interview with a girl called Sophie and a boy called Marc. For each question, circle the correct option **a**, **b** or **c**.

1 What type of food are they talking about?
   a pizza   **b** cheese   **c** chicken
2 What does Sophie think of Roquefort?
   a She thinks it is horrible.
   b She thinks it is strange.
   c She thinks it is delicious.
3 Where is Roquefort made?
   a in the south of France
   b in the north of France
   c in the south of Spain
4 When was it discovered?
   a in 97 AD   **b** in 1709 AD   **c** in 79 AD

Exam Reminder

Listening for numbers

• Remember to read the questions carefully and make sure you understand the topic before you listen.
• Underline any important words, numbers and dates in the questions and answer options.
• Remember to be careful with dates and numbers because they can sound very similar. Check your answers carefully when you listen the second time.

5 What is it made from?
   a sheep   **b** sheep's milk   **c** eggs
6 Where do they leave the cheese for three months?
   a in caves
   b on the fields by the mountains
   c with the shepherds

C `2.1` ▷ Listen again and check your answers.

Vocabulary

A Complete the sentences with these words.

> bright   choose   decide   mixing   trendy   variety

1 What are you going to _____ for your starter?
2 I can't _____ between the salad and the chicken.
3 There's such a great _____ of cupcakes in that bakery.
4 Sweetcorn is usually a _____ yellow colour.
5 The Italian restaurant at the end of my road is really _____. It's modern and very popular.
6 You make a cake by _____ eggs, flour, sugar and butter together.

B Circle the correct words.

Another bad day for Basil!

Basil was worried. It was another bad day at the **(1)** tradition / traditional café he owned. The café didn't have very many **(2)** customary / customers. He had to **(3)** decisive / decide what to do. 'Why didn't I open a **(4)** trendy / trend burger place instead?' he asked himself. 'A place with **(5)** colourful / colour chairs and tables and a **(6)** choose / choice of different kinds of burgers.' Basil would have to do something, otherwise his business would close.

Grammar

used to & would; be used to & get used to

A Complete the dialogues with one word in each gap.

1 **A:** I have to get _____ to my new diet. What about you?
   B: Oh, no problems. I _____ used to it now.

2 **A:** Did you _____ to drink coffee when you were younger?
   B: No, I _____ not!

3 **A:** We _____ always go fishing on Sundays when I was young.
   B: Really? We didn't use _____ do anything.

4 **A:** How's the new job? Are you _____ to working at night now?
   B: Well, I'm _____ used to it, I suppose.

B Find and circle the eight mistakes in the text below.

Ancient fast food

We think of fast food as modern, but the truth is that fast food has been around for thousands of years! Recent excavations at Pompeii, Italy, indicate that people didn't used to cook at home. Many of the houses didn't have kitchens, pots, pans, plates, bowls or cups. Also, archaeologists used to find evidence of ancient restaurants. The buildings would opening to the street and would had large kitchen areas in the back and service areas at the front. More amazing, however, is that these buildings wouldn't have any tables, chairs or space to sit down. The service areas being at the front of the restaurant and, clearly, people use to walk up to the service area, order their food, pay for it and go. Much like our fast food restaurants today!

Use your English

A Complete the text with the correct form of the words.

The World's Best Restaurant

Year after year, *El Bulli* in Spain has won the award for the world's best restaurant. It opens for six months a year, only for dinner and only for 50 people a night. The amazing thing is that (1) _____ 800,000 people call or email for a table every season!

APPROXIMATE
TREND

What makes *El Bulli* so (2) _____ ? Its chef, Ferran Adrià, does amazing things with food. During the winter months, he spends his time in a laboratory instead of a kitchen and it's there that he creates (3) _____ new dishes. He experiments with ingredients to see what happens when they are grilled, baked or (4) _____ and he is famous for transforming (5) _____ recipes. Food critics say that his food and flavours are very imaginative. He really is the king of (6) _____ restaurants!

TASTE
FRY
TRADITION
EXPENSE
HUNGER

But if you're (7) _____ for incredible food, check your wallet first. A meal at *El Bulli* costs around 250 euros per person. For that you get 30 small courses made up of a (8) _____ of meat, fish, seafood and vegetable dishes, as well as desserts. It's sure to be unforgettable!

VARIOUS

Writing: a review

Ordering adjectives
- When you have two or more adjectives before a noun, you must write them in the correct order: opinion, size, shape, age, colour, origin and material.
- Don't forget to use *and* between two adjectives of the same kind and to put them in alphabetical order.

A Circle the odd one out. Then, on the left, write the correct name of the group and, on the right, add one more adjective of your own to each group.

1 _____ :	new	special	ancient	_____
2 _____ :	strong	long	round	_____
3 _____ :	French	European	Greece	_____
4 _____ :	incredible	tiny	awful	_____
5 _____ :	bright	leather	cotton	_____
6 _____ :	black	yellow	old	_____
7 _____ :	little	silk	huge	_____

B Read the writing task below and then correct the statements.

You recently went to a new café in town and you were very impressed. Write a review of the café for your school magazine giving your opinion and saying why you would recommend it.

1 You didn't like the new café. _____
2 You will write to your friend about the café. _____
3 You will say what other people think of the café. _____
4 You will say negative things about the café. _____

C Read the example review and complete it with these nouns. Can you think of one more adjective for each of the nouns in the wordbank?

cheese   coffee   flowers   food   pictures   sandwich   tomatoes   waiters

Casbah Café: The best coffee and snacks in town!

Do you hang out at cafés with your friends? If you do, try the Casbah Café! At the Casbah, you'll get fresh, tasty (1) _____ and fantastic Italian coffee for less!

> Introduce what you are reviewing

The Casbah only opened a few weeks ago, but it has already become extremely popular. And I can see why. I ordered a sandwich with juicy red (2) _____, creamy white mozzarella (3) _____ and delicious pesto sauce. The (4) _____ was huge and very filling. I had a strong black (5) _____ to drink and it was full of flavour.

> Describe the meal you ate.

You'll love the Casbah. There are trendy, colourful (6) _____ on the walls and lovely, fresh (7) _____ on the tables. The (8) _____ were very friendly and helpful, and the service was quick, even though the place was full of customers. There was a lot to choose from on the menu and it was really cheap.

> Give details about the restaurant or café.

The delicious food and drinks, good prices and welcoming atmosphere make the Casbah Café the hottest place in town. I highly recommend it to all teenagers.

> Give your opinion of the restaurant or café and make a recommendation.

D Read and complete the *Exam Task* below. Don't forget to use the *Useful Expressions* on page 27 of your Student's Book.

Exam Task

A group of teenagers from another country is coming to visit your town. Your teacher has asked you to recommend a place for them to eat. Write a **review** of a café or restaurant. Give your opinion and say why you would recommend it to others. (100 words)

Writing Reference p. 180 in Student's Book

Vocabulary

A **Choose the correct answers.**

1 Aunt Sally has beautiful eyes, so people always ___ her compliments.

   a say   **c** make

   b pay   **d** have

2 My grandfather got ___ in France because his wife is French.

   a love   **c** married

   b family   **d** sympathy

3 Dad is looking for his ___ by researching his family tree.

   a generations   **c** ancestors

   b genes   **d** histories

4 Joe's ___ grandparents are both over 90, but they still love to go walking.

   a middle-aged   **c** scruffy

   b arrogant   **d** elderly

5 My aunt is very ___. She always does what she says she will do.

   a generous   **c** hard-working

   b jealous   **d** reliable

6 She put the spoons in the drawer with the ___.

   a fridge   **c** kitchen

   b knives   **d** dessert

7 You are always busy and you are so hard-working. You need to ___ more.

   a weigh   **c** build

   b relax   **d** lazy

8 'How long have you been married?'

'I'm not married any more. We got ___ last year.'

   a married   **c** divorced

   b moved   **d** overweight

9 My cousin is very ___, but she eats a lot. It's very strange!

   a tall   **c** slim

   b overweight   **d** weigh

10 'Why don't you have some cake?'

'I'm not very ___, but thanks.'

   a tasty   **c** thirsty

   b delicious   **d** hungry

11 My parents act like they are still young, but really they're ___. It's embarrassing.

   a middle-aged   **c** hard-working

   b overweight   **d** easy-going

12 Jane can't stop eating junk food so she is a bit ___.

   a overweight   **c** weight

   b build   **d** slim

13 The burger was absolutely ___. I want my money back, please!

   a tasty   **c** trendy

   b tasteless   **d** delicious

14 You'll need a knife to ___ the aubergine.

   a boil   **c** chew

   b chop   **d** bite

15 'You look too young to have a teenage son.'

'Well, I got married young and ___ a family straight away.'

   a made   **c** created

   b did   **d** had

16 This traditional ___ is made with vegetables and cheese.

   a jug   **c** dessert

   b starter   **d** bowl

17 My sister is very ___. She always helps people who have a problem.

   a blonde   **c** kind

   b jealous   **d** honest

18 I've got the same ___ as my grandfather. We're both short and slim.

   a weigh   **c** build

   b overweight   **d** height

19 I can't ___ between the chocolate or the strawberry cupcake.

   a decision   **c** decisive

   b decide   **d** decided

20 The ___ of fruit in the supermarket is fantastic.

   a various   **c** variety

   b variously   **d** vary

Grammar

B Choose the correct answers.

1 'Isn't that your uncle over there?'
'Well, he ___, but he and my aunt got divorced last year.'

   a used to be   **c** was being

   b would be   **d** was used to

2 We don't serve chips in the school canteen because ___ parents think they're unhealthy.

   a a little   **c** lots of

   b few   **d** much

3 Mum ___ breakfast, so she doesn't feel hungry before lunch.

   a is always having **c** always is having

   b has always   **d** always has

4 If you've only got ___ money left, we can recommend a very good, but cheap, restaurant.

   a a little   **c** many

   b a few   **d** much

5 'Have you got any plans for Saturday night?'
'Yes, ___ to a family party for my grandmother's 70th birthday.'

   a I'm going   **c** I used to go

   b I go   **d** I would go

6 'Shall we try the new café in town tomorrow?'
'Yes, but it ___ until noon.'

   a opens   **c** opened

   b doesn't open **d** is opening

7 When I was living in this town, I ___ my aunt every Saturday.

   a used to visiting **c** am visiting

   b was visiting   **d** would visit

8 When Ben first tried the diet, it was hard because he ___ eating so little.

   a wasn't used to **c** used to

   b was used to   **d** didn't use to

9 Jane ___ a cake for Penny's birthday party every year.

   a is making   **c** was made

   b was making   **d** makes

10 'Do you like my cooking, John?'
'I'm ___.'

   a being used to it **c** getting used to it

   b get used to it   **d** used to doing it

11 Children ___ usually upset when their parents get divorced.

   a are   **c** are being

   b is   **d** would be

12 'What are you making? It ___ really delicious.'
'I'm making a chocolate cake.'

   a smells   **c** was smelling

   b is smelling   **d** smelt

13 Uncle Mike was listening to music while he ___ the burgers.

   a is frying   **c** would fry

   b used to fry   **d** was frying

14 My daughter ___ to like that dish, but now it's her favourite!

   a isn't used   **c** got used

   b was used   **d** didn't use

15 When Lisa was a child, she hated vegetables and ___ eat them.

   a wouldn't   **c** used

   b didn't use   **d** wasn't used

16 Harry ___ late for school because he eats his breakfast so slowly.

   a usually is   **c** usually is being

   b is usually   **d** is being usually

17 Sherry ___ it hard to make new friends at the moment.

   a 's finding   **c** found

   b would find   **d** used to find

18 Penny ___ of getting her children a dog.

   a thinks   **c** is thinking

   b used to think **d** didn't use to think

19 I'm going to the shops. Should I get ___ loaf of bread?

   a some   **c** a

   b an   **d** much

20 Would you like ___ fruit, Maria?

   a a   **c** some

   b an   **d** many

Reading

A Read the *Exam Reminder*. What can help you understand text types?

_____

B Now complete the *Exam Task*.

Danger at the ends of the Earth

Welcome to Nunavik – a beautiful landscape of forests, blue skies and clear waters. It's a huge area with 14 Inuit villages in the Arctic area of Canada. Wild animals, such as bears and wolves, can be seen everywhere. There are also caribou (a kind of reindeer), and fish fill the rivers, lakes and sea. In summer, the sun shines day and night, and so this is when the people fish, hunt and pick berries. Winter is cold and dark, but at night, stars fill the clear, dark sky and you can often even see the Northern Lights. You might think that Nunavik's geographical position at the ends of the Earth keeps it safe from big city problems like air and water pollution. Unfortunately, the pretty villages of Nunavik have not escaped the problems that the rest of the world is facing, too.

Some years ago, scientists made a worrying discovery. An extremely dangerous group of chemicals known as 'persistent organic pollutants' (or POPs) were attacking the Arctic environment. There are few factories there and not many cars, so where was the pollution coming from? It turns out that it was coming from cities thousands of kilometres away. But how?

POPs are used everywhere – in TVs, in lights and in paint. They are also sprayed onto crops as pesticides. Over time, they become gas and go into the air, and the wind carries them thousands of kilometres. When they reach a cold environment, the gas becomes a liquid, like water. So when the wind carries POPs into the Arctic, cold temperatures make them stick to plants and fall into the oceans, where they stay and increase over time. POPs also collect inside the fat of people and animals, and they stay there forever. The biggest animals, like seals and whales, have the most POPs in their bodies. These are the animals that Inuit people have been eating for thousands of years.

POPs can cause cancer and allergies, as well as other damage. They can also cause developmental problems in babies and children. Clearly, something had to be done about the problem and so in the 1990s, the United Nations held a meeting called the Stockholm Convention to discuss banning lots of the POP chemicals. Since then, many countries have agreed to start producing fewer POP chemicals, and as a result, levels of POPs in the Arctic are falling.

It will take many years for the problem to go away. For one thing, buildings around the world still have many tons of POPs in their paint and wiring. Every day, those chemicals turn into gas and enter the atmosphere, eventually reaching the Arctic.

For the Inuit people, and all the people and animals in the Arctic regions, their only hope is the work of scientists and the help of the rest of the world in putting an end to POPs once and for all.

Exam Task

Read the text and questions below. For each question, choose the correct letter **a**, **b**, **c** or **d**.

1 What is the writer doing with this text?
- **a** entertaining the reader
- **b** giving information about the Arctic and POPs
- **c** describing Nunavik
- **d** persuading people to visit the Arctic

2 What is true about the Inuit people according to the article?
- **a** They all have health problems.
- **b** Many of them drive cars.
- **c** They find their food in nature.
- **d** They eat a lot of fat.

3 How do POPs get to the Arctic?
- **a** Other countries send them there.
- **b** They are in the oceans.
- **c** Factories in the Arctic produce them.
- **d** They are carried in the atmosphere.

4 What effect has the Stockholm Convention had?
- **a** The United Nations solved the problem in 1990.
- **b** POP chemicals have been banned.
- **c** The level of POP chemicals is reducing.
- **d** The Inuit people have more health problems.

5 Which is the best summary of the text?
- **a** Animals are facing many problems in the Arctic.
- **b** POP chemicals are causing environmental problems in the Arctic.
- **c** The Stockholm Convention is deciding the world's future.
- **d** The United Nations wants to help the environment.

Vocabulary

A Choose the correct answers.

1 It was quite dark inside the ___ in Iceland.
   a coast   b cave   c cliff

2 There were brightly-coloured fish swimming in the ___.
   a pond   b cave   c valley

3 We need to protect the ___ before all the trees are destroyed.
   a cliffs   b caves   c rainforests

4 ___ are melting because our climate is changing.
   a Glaciers   b Ponds   c Streams

5 Solar ___ is a renewable energy.
   a habitats   b fuels   c power

6 We must take action in order to prevent ___ change.
   a energy   b climate   c conservation

B Complete the sentences with these collocations.

climate change   conservation areas   endangered species   fossil fuels
natural habitat   power station   renewable energy   solar power

1 Wind power is a form of _____ that we should be using.
2 Most people agree that _____ is a big problem for humans today.
3 Polar bears are a(n) _____ because their natural habitat is disappearing.
4 Some countries have created _____ for endangered animals to live in.
5 _____ include things such as coal, oil and natural gas.
6 Light and heat from the sun is used to produce _____.
7 The air around the _____ was dirty and it gave me a headache.
8 The _____ of the penguin is icy Antarctica.

Grammar

Present Perfect Simple; Present Perfect Continuous

A Complete the text by writing one word in each gap.

South American Adventure

Simon (1) _____ been travelling. Read about his last trip here …

'I haven't visited Asia (2) _____, but I (3) _____ travelled to South America a number of times. The last time I went to South America was a month (4) _____. I visited Brazil, Venezuela and Argentina. I spent two weeks in the Amazon. It was incredible! I made a lot of videos. I have (5) _____ telling all of my friends about the amazing things I saw. I have been back in London (6) _____ last Friday and I'm already planning my next trip!'

B Complete the sentences with the Present Perfect Simple, the Present Perfect Continuous or the Past Simple. Use the verbs given.

1 lose
   Last night I _____ my dog, but my sister found him.
   I _____ my dog. Can you help me look for him?

2 work
   I _____ on my project all night; that's why I'm tired.
   I _____ on my project all day yesterday.

3 visit
   The scientist _____ Antarctica three times.
   Last year the scientist _____ Antarctica.

4 go
   Jim _____ to the zoo yesterday.
   Jim isn't here now. He _____ to the zoo.

5 wait
   I _____ for you for hours! Why are you late?
   I _____ for you for an hour and then I left.

6 have
   I _____ a motorbike for a few years, but then I sold it.
   I _____ this motorbike for years and it's still working.

Listening

A Read the *Exam Reminder*. How many words will you write in each gap?

_____

B 🔊 **3.1** ▶️❚❚ Listen and complete the *Exam Task*.

Exam Task

You will hear some information about water. For each question, fill in the missing information in the numbered space.

Water for Africa

Number of litres of water a day needed to survive: **(1)** _____
Strange effects on weather because of: **(2)** _____
Who / What extreme weather is damaging: **(3)** _____

Reason why many people can't grow food: **(4)** _____
Name of charity: **(5)** _____
Charity has provided 22,500 people with: **(6)** _____

Exam Reminder

Thinking about the answers first
- Remember to try to identify what type of information should go in each gap before listening.
- First, look at the words before and after each gap to decide which type of word or number could fit in the gap.
- Next, listen and write the words you hear. You will probably need to write between one and three words in each gap.

C 🔊 **3.1** ▶️❚❚ Listen again and check your answers.

Vocabulary

A Complete the dialogues with these prepositions.

> after   at   from   in   on   over

1 **A:** Can I speak to you about something?
   B: Yes, of course, but I'm busy _____ the moment. How about later?
2 **A:** _____ weeks of planning, we have finally cleaned up the beach.
   B: Yes, we worked hard for _____ five hours, but it looks great now.
3 **A:** This article says that dangerous chemicals are appearing _____ our food.
   B: Yes, they're everywhere – _____ meat and fish to fruit and vegetables.
4 **A:** Oh no! They're going to build a motorway next to our school!
   B: Yes, I know. We need to take action _____ it now before it's too late.

B Read the *Exam Reminder* and complete the *Exam Task*.

Exam Task

Read the text below and choose the correct word for each space. For each question, mark the correct letter **a**, **b**, **c** or **d**.

The largest desert in the world

What does the word 'desert' make you think of? Do you imagine a hot, sandy place such as the Sahara in Africa? That's what most people think of, but did you know that Antarctica is the largest desert in the world? A desert is any place that has less than 2.5 cm of water a year, and Antarctica has less than that. Antarctica is made up of 98% ice and 2% rock. The ice is mainly in the form of glaciers. If these glaciers melt because of global warming, the ice will turn **(1)** _____ water, the sea level will rise and cities on the coasts will be covered by water. **(2)** _____ the moment, Antarctica is the home of the Emperor Penguin, but if the ice melts, its home will start to disappear and it will become an endangered species. After centuries **(3)** _____ living on the ice, Emperor Penguins could find themselves at risk. This risk is very real and scientists say we need to take action **(4)** _____ this issue. We must do something about global warming **(5)** _____ it's too late.

Exam Reminder

Reading a multiple-choice text first
- Remember to read all the text first before you try to complete it.
- Read the text to check you have a general understanding of what it is about before you choose the answers.
- Read the text again and check it makes sense after you have chosen the answers.

1 **a** into   **b** onto   **c** from   **d** in
2 **a** After   **b** In   **c** Before   **d** At
3 **a** on   **b** at   **c** of   **d** for
4 **a** in   **b** on   **c** for   **d** at
5 **a** from   **b** for   **c** after   **d** before

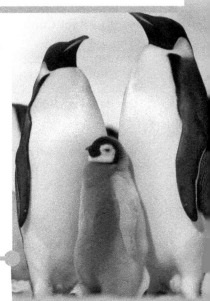

Grammar

Articles

A Circle the correct words.

1 Have you ever been to the / - United Kingdom?
2 Climate change is a / the problem everyone has to take action on.
3 I think - / the dolphins are very intelligent creatures.
4 The / A polar bear is - / an endangered species.
5 I was amazed by the colours of - / the fish in the / an pond.
6 An / A conservation area is the / an best place for endangered animals to live.

B Complete the text with *a*, *the*, or -.

The Grand Canyon

Have you ever been to (1) _____ Grand Canyon? It's (2) _____ World Heritage site and one of (3) _____ world's most impressive geological areas.

It was formed by (4) _____ Colorado River as it flowed across (5) _____ land. The process started 17 million years ago and it has continued since then.

There are many ways to explore this amazing place. Helicopters can take you through (6) _____ valleys, or you can hike in (7) _____ other areas. There is also (8) _____ skywalk. (9) _____ skywalk is 1,200 metres above the river and it's got (10) _____ glass floor, so you can see all the way down into the canyon. Don't try it if you're scared of heights!

Use your English

A Complete the second sentences so that they have a similar meaning to the first sentences, using the words in bold. Use between two and five words.

1 I met Kate eight years ago and we're still good friends.
   known
   I _____ eight years.

2 We began our trip in Scotland and finished it in Wales.
   from
   We have travelled _____ Wales.

3 Robert teaches biology at a high school.
   teacher
   Robert is _____ at a high school.

4 I got here at one o'clock and it's now three o'clock.
   for
   I _____ two hours.

5 Beth went to the library and she's still there.
   has
   Beth _____ to the library.

6 People must do something about climate change.
   take
   We must _____ climate change.

7 Karen started studying at five o'clock.
   been
   Karen _____ five o'clock.

8 The film finished at six o'clock and it's half past six now.
   half
   The film finished _____ ago.

Writing: an informal email

A Complete the table with these expressions.

> Bye!   Bye for now.   Hello.   Hi!   How are you?
> How are things?   How is it going?   See you soon.
> Speak to you later.   That's all for now.   Write soon!

Starting an email or letter	Ending an email or letter

Including useful expressions

- Remember that useful expressions can make an informal letter or email sound more natural.
- You can start a letter or email with friendly questions and greetings, e.g. *Hi! How are you?*
- You can end a letter or email with friendly expressions, e.g. *Bye for now! Speak to you later.*
- You can also use other expressions in informal letters and emails, e.g. *Sorry for not answering your last email. Good luck!*

B Read the writing task below and then decide if the statements are true (T) or false (F).

This is part of an email you get from a friend in England.

> Our teacher has asked the class to write about recycling in schools. I want to write about what people do at your school. Can you send me some information?

Now write an email to your friend.

1 You have to write a letter. ☐
2 The text will be about recycling at home. ☐
3 Your friend needs some information. ☐
4 The email will be informal. ☐

C Read the example email and circle the correct words.

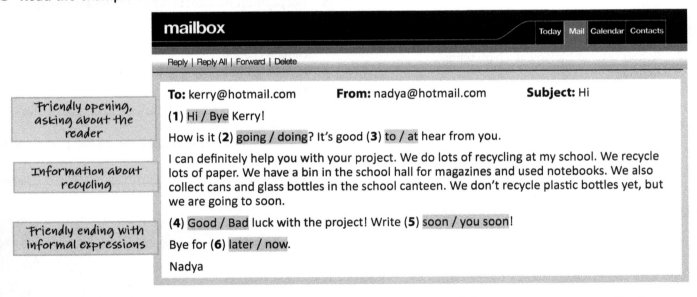

Friendly opening, asking about the reader

Information about recycling

Friendly ending with informal expressions

mailbox   Today | Mail | Calendar | Contacts

Reply | Reply All | Forward | Delete

To: kerry@hotmail.com   **From:** nadya@hotmail.com   **Subject:** Hi

(1) Hi / Bye Kerry!

How is it **(2)** going / doing? It's good **(3)** to / at hear from you.

I can definitely help you with your project. We do lots of recycling at my school. We recycle lots of paper. We have a bin in the school hall for magazines and used notebooks. We also collect cans and glass bottles in the school canteen. We don't recycle plastic bottles yet, but we are going to soon.

(4) Good / Bad luck with the project! Write **(5)** soon / you soon!

Bye for **(6)** later / now.

Nadya

D Read and complete the *Exam Task* below. Don't forget to use the *Useful Expressions* on page 41 of your Student's Book.

Exam Task

This is part of an email you get from a friend in England.

> We are doing a project at school about conservation areas around the world. I want to make mine about an area in your country. Can you send me some information about it?

Now write an **email** to your friend. (100 words)

↪ **Writing Reference** p. 177 in Student's Book

Reading

A Read the *Exam Reminder*. What can help you identify the meaning of new words?

_____

B Now complete the *Exam Task*.

Animal bravery

Some pets have shown astonishing courage in dangerous situations and have saved the lives of their owners. Here, we tell you about four amazing animals.

A Selvakumar, India
Selvakumar looks like every other dog in the south Indian village where he lives. An obedient family pet, he plays with the children, sleeps with the family and goes with seven-year-old Dinakaran to and from school. The events of December 26, 2004, however, proved that Selvakumar isn't just an ordinary dog. That was the day a huge tsunami hit the coast around the Indian Ocean, including the village where Selvakumar and his owners lived. Most of the family had managed to run away from the water, but Dinakaran went to the family's hut, which was only metres from the seashore. Selvakumar ran into the hut after the boy. Pushing with his teeth, he managed to get the boy up the hill and saved his life.

B Lulu, Australia
Lulu, the pet kangaroo, was rescued by the Richards family after her mother had been killed by a car. Lulu returned the favour one day when she helped save the life of her owner, Australian farmer, Len Richards. During a storm, a falling tree knocked Len unconscious. Lulu quickly hopped home and made a noise so Len's wife, Lynn, would hear her. She looked for her husband and found him in a field. Amazingly, it appeared that Lulu had pushed Len onto his side when he began being sick, which had saved him from choking. Due to her bravery, Lulu was the first kangaroo to receive an animal bravery award.

C Gepetto, Canada
Winter in Canada is difficult. Early one December morning in 2009, Phyllis Sjogren woke up feeling very cold. She turned the heating up and went back to bed. Phyllis noticed she had a strong headache, but just ignored it. Later that morning, she was woken up by her cat, Gepetto.

By now, Phyllis felt dizzy and had trouble walking. She comforted Gepetto because he seemed upset, and then called her husband to tell him what was happening. Realising what the problem was, Martin Sjogren told his wife to leave the house immediately. So what was the problem? Their home had filled with carbon monoxide gas overnight, which cannot be seen nor smelt, but can cause death. Gepetto had saved Phyllis's life.

D LuLu, USA
On a hot August day, Jo Ann Altsman had a heart attack in the bedroom of her holiday home. After she collapsed, her dog began to bark loudly, but no one heard him. Then LuLu, her lovely pot-bellied pig, took control of the situation. Pushing herself through a small doggie door, where she cut her stomach, LuLu waited by the road until a car approached. Then, she walked onto the road and lay down in front of the car. The driver stopped and got out. LuLu led the man to the

house, where he called an ambulance so that Jo Ann was saved. Many people believe that pigs are more intelligent than dogs and Jo Ann most certainly agrees!

Look at the sentences below about brave animals. Read the text to decide if each sentence is correct or incorrect. Write **T** (True) or **F** (False).

1 Selvakumar looks different from the other dogs in his village. ☐
2 Selvakumar's family have a hut on the beach. ☐
3 Selvakumar pushed Dinakaran to safety. ☐
4 Len's mother was run over by a car. ☐
5 Phyllis was worried about her headache. ☐
6 Martin knew there was carbon monoxide in the house. ☐

7 You can smell carbon monoxide. ☐
8 LuLu injured her stomach on the road. ☐
9 The driver followed LuLu to the house. ☐
10 Jo Ann thinks pigs are less intelligent than dogs. ☐

Vocabulary

A Complete the sentences with *on*, *with*, *of* or *to*.

1 When you have a problem, don't worry. Concentrate _____ finding a solution.
2 I can't believe Charlotte is in love _____ Mike. I thought she didn't even like him.
3 Dan is quite similar _____ his dad. They are both slim and have brown hair.
4 I bought a kitten without asking my parents and now my mum is angry _____ me.
5 My mum doesn't mind leaving our dog, but my dad doesn't agree _____ her, so we always take him on holiday.
6 My sister is not very keen _____ chocolate; she prefers fruit.
7 James is really jealous _____ Sophie because she is very intelligent.
8 If you have a problem, you can rely _____ your friend to help you.

B Complete the text with these words.

belong concentrate listen proud rely similar

The first day of school

The first day of school can be a very difficult time for teenagers. There are so many new things: new teachers, new friends and maybe even a new school. There are fears about making friends. Will you find friends you are (1) _____ to? Will there be people you can (2) _____ on if you need help with something? But don't worry too much. Be yourself and your parents will be (3) _____ of you. Don't become friends with people you don't like just because you want to (4) _____ to a group.

Don't forget to (5) _____ to the teachers. They are giving you important information and it is important to (6) _____ on what they say.

Finally, relax and enjoy your first day!

Grammar

Relative Clauses: defining & non-defining

A Choose the correct answers.

1 Annie sometimes feeds the cats ___ live in her neighbourhood.
   a where   b whose   c that

2 Is that the student ___ essay won the competition?
   a which   b whose   c that

3 I think people ___ have pets have happier lives!
   a which   b who   c when

4 That's the youth club ___ all the teenagers go after school.
   a who   b that   c where

5 I'm looking forward to the day ___ I go to university.
   a when   b where   c which

6 Their uncle, ___ cat ran away, is very upset.
   a who   b that   c whose

B Tick (✓) the sentences that are correct. Rewrite the incorrect sentences.

1 That's the man who built our new house in the countryside. _____
2 The bus where goes to the station will be here soon. _____
3 My friend, who mother is a doctor, is very good at biology. _____
4 A stadium is a place which people play sports. _____
5 The bridge, where we cross the river, isn't far from here. _____
6 Winter is the time of year where we don't go out a lot. _____
7 Jenny, who lives next door, is very nice. _____
8 The café, when is on the corner, is popular with teens. _____

Listening

A Read the *Exam Reminder*. Should you read the questions or listen first?

_____

Exam Reminder

Listening for similar words

- Remember that you won't hear the same words that you read in the questions.
- Listen for similar words that describe how people think and feel.
- Before you listen, try to think of similar words to those on the exam question.

B 4.1 ▶❙❙ Listen and complete the *Exam Task*.

Exam Task

Look at the six sentences for this part. You will hear a conversation between a girl, Kate, and a boy, Charlie, about Kate's time at university. Decide if each sentence is correct or incorrect. Write **T** (True) or **F** (False).

1 In her first year, Kate spent all her time studying at home or in the library. ☐
2 Kate chose to study two subjects at university; history and art. ☐
3 Kate's old school friends had started doing lots of new activities at their universities. ☐
4 Her decision to live with other students took a lot of courage. ☐
5 She found out that she and the other students didn't share any interests. ☐
6 Kate has now started doing some new active hobbies. ☐

C 4.1 ▶❙❙ Listen again and check your answers.

Vocabulary

A Match the first parts of the sentences 1–6 to the second parts a–f.

1 Lisa really looks ☐
2 I really enjoy working with Penny on the project. We get ☐
3 Have you heard the news? Brad broke ☐
4 The girls from school like hanging ☐
5 James had a big argument with his best friend, but they made ☐
6 I don't like Stacey any more. She always puts ☐

a up with Elena last night and she's really upset.
b me down and it makes me really upset.
c up the next day.
d up to her big sister. She would like to be like her when she is older.
e out at the park at the weekend.
f on so well and never argue.

B Replace the underlined words with these phrasal verbs in the correct form.

> ask someone out   break up with   get on   hang out
> let someone down   look up to   make up   put someone down

1 We had an argument, but then we <u>forgave each other</u>. _____
2 The students <u>have a lot of respect for</u> their head teacher. _____
3 I like <u>spending time</u> with my friends during breaks at school. _____
4 I'm so sorry that I <u>disappointed you</u>. _____
5 Harry's too shy to <u>invite Mary on a date</u>. _____
6 Sara has decided to <u>stop being Tom's girlfriend</u> so she has more time to study. _____
7 I hope I can <u>be friends</u> with the people in my new school. _____
8 A teacher must never <u>make pupils feel stupid</u>. _____

Grammar

Temporals

A Choose the sentence (a or b) which means the same as the first sentence.

1 The fans will leave as soon as the concert finishes.
  a The fans will leave and then the concert will finish.
  b The concert will finish and then the fans will leave.

2 When I go to high school, I'll make new friends.
  a I will make new friends and then go to high school.
  b I will go to high school and then make new friends.

3 Let's stay until the film ends.
  a The film will end and then we will go home.
  b We will go home and then the film will end.

4 Make sure you have enough money before you go out.
  a Go out and then check your purse.
  b Check your purse and then go out.

5 He fell in love the moment he saw her.
  a He saw her and then he fell in love.
  b He fell in love and then he saw her.

6 By the time you get my letter, I will be in France.
  a I will go to France and then you will get my letter.
  b You will get my letter and then I will go to France.

B Complete the text with these words.

as soon   before   the moment   until

The zebra and the oxpecker bird

A symbiotic relationship is a relationship between two living things of different species which help each other. One example of a symbiotic relationship is the oxpecker bird and the zebra. Oxpeckers sit on zebras looking for insects. **(1)** _____ as they find some, they eat them. In this way, the oxpeckers get food and the zebras get rid of annoying pests! Also, **(2)** _____ there is danger, the oxpeckers fly away while making a very loud noise, which helps the zebra spot the problem **(3)** _____ it gets too serious. Then the oxpeckers stay away **(4)** _____ the danger passes. It's a relationship that benefits both animals!

Use your English

A Choose the correct answers.

When friendships end

Most friendships slowly come to an end over time. Other friendships, however, end very suddenly. Sometimes a friend might end your relationship without telling you why.

When a friendship ends, try to work out why it has ended. Maybe you did things **(1)** _____ annoyed your friend. Perhaps your friend felt you **(2)** _____ them down or that they couldn't rely **(3)** _____ you when they needed help.

Whatever the reasons for the split, don't be **(4)** _____ with them. You never know – there may come a time in the future **(5)** _____ you and your friend make **(6)** _____, and you don't want to say anything now **(7)** _____ you might regret later.

1	**a**	who	**b**	where	**c**	that	**d**	when
2	**a**	made	**b**	let	**c**	broke	**d**	looked
3	**a**	with	**b**	on	**c**	for	**d**	to
4	**a**	jealous	**b**	angry	**c**	ashamed	**d**	proud
5	**a**	that	**b**	when	**c**	which	**d**	where
6	**a**	up	**b**	with	**c**	for	**d**	to
7	**a**	whose	**b**	when	**c**	who	**d**	which

Writing: a story (1)

A Match the first parts of the sentences 1–3 to the second parts a–c.

1 The beginning of a story ☐
2 The middle of a story ☐
3 The end of a story ☐

a explains the action in the story.
b introduces and describes the time, people and location of a story.
c describes the action in the story.

Learning Reminder

Organising a story

- Remember that most stories have a beginning, middle and end.
- The beginning introduces the people, place and time of the story.
- The middle describes what happens in the story. It usually has several paragraphs and sometimes includes something surprising or unexpected.
- The end explains the events of the story or leaves what happens in the end as a mystery.

B Read the writing task below and then decide if the statements are true (T) or false (F).

Your English teacher has asked you to write a story. Your story must have this title: A strange day.

1 You need to write an email. ☐
2 You can begin your story any way you like. ☐
3 The story will be about a strange year. ☐

C Read the example story below and then answer the questions about it.

Emma woke up. The sun was shining outside and she felt good. It was the last day of school and she was going on holiday tomorrow.

She got dressed and went downstairs for breakfast. There was some orange juice and some cereal on the table, but her parents were nowhere to be seen. 'Perhaps they went to work early,' Emma thought.

So Emma ate her breakfast and then left the house. The streets were very quiet and she didn't see any cars or people. 'That's strange,' thought Emma. 'I wonder where everyone is?'

When Emma arrived at school, she went to her classroom. There was nobody there! She looked around the whole school, but she couldn't find anyone. Suddenly, Emma was scared. What had happened to everyone? Was she the only person left on the planet?

She ran all the way back home and opened the door. The first thing she saw was her mother standing at the top of the stairs, wearing her pyjamas. She looked worried.

'Emma, where have you been?' she said. 'I've been at school,' Emma said, 'but there was nobody there. There was nobody anywhere!'

'School?' said Emma's mum. 'But it's five o'clock in the morning! Has your clock broken again?'

1 Who is the main character? _____
2 Where is the story set? _____
3 Are there any other characters? _____
4 Something strange happens. What is it? _____
5 How does the story end? _____

D Read and complete the *Exam Task* below. Don't forget to use the *Useful Expressions* on page 53 of your Student's Book.

Exam Task

Your English teacher has asked you to write a **story**. Your story must begin with this sentence: *Hannah woke up and realised something.* (100 words)

↻ Writing Reference p. 179 in Student's Book

Vocabulary

A Choose the correct answers.

1 Governments must do something about pollution ___ it's too late.

   a after   **c** before

   b across   **d** from

2 There are very few tigers in the world; it is an ___ species.

   a endangered   **c** renewable

   b conservation   **d** natural

3 The natural ___ of this species of turtle is the Aegean Sea.

   a balance   **c** survival

   b habitat   **d** resource

4 ___ energy comes from wind, water and other natural sources.

   a Fossil   **c** Renewable

   b Solar   **d** Natural

5 Come away from the edge! Someone fell off that ___ last week!

   a cave   **c** rainforest

   b coast   **d** cliff

6 The ___ is disappearing very quickly. We have to do something to stop it.

   a glaciers   **c** stream

   b rainforest   **d** valley

7 The teenagers ran ___ one end of the beach to the other.

   a between   **c** from

   b across   **d** for

8 It is now possible to turn old cooking oil ___ fuel for cars.

   a to   **c** up

   b on   **d** into

9 He was a loving husband and father, and he was very ___ of his family.

   a proud   **c** jealous

   b similar   **d** keen

10 Jake often hangs ___ with his brother at school.

   a to   **c** for

   b out   **d** on

11 I can't talk right now. I'm very busy ___ the moment.

   a for   **c** from

   b at   **d** around

12 Kevin doesn't like his cousin, who is always ___ him down.

   a putting   **c** looking

   b making   **d** taking

13 ___ months of hard work, we've finally managed to clean up the city's parks.

   a Between   **c** Over

   b Across   **d** After

14 They believe the walkers entered the dark ___ and got lost.

   a cave   **c** pond

   b cliff   **d** stream

15 Steve really looks ___ to his grandfather. He admires him a lot.

   a on   **c** at

   b for   **d** up

16 Paul and his girlfriend used to get on well, but they ___ up last week.

   a broke   **c** got

   b put   **d** let

17 My dream is to live on the ___ of Scotland.

   a coast   **c** rainforest

   b cliff   **d** glacier

18 I spend a lot of time ___ out with my friends.

   a breaking   **c** looking

   b hanging   **d** letting

Grammar

B Choose the correct answers.

1 The Amazon rainforest, ___ is in South America, is disappearing fast.
   a when   **c** where
   b which   **d** who

2 'Is Jackie a friend of yours?'
  'Yes, I ___ her for years.'
   a have been knowing
   b knew
   c know
   d have known

3 'Why is Sam looking so happy?'
  'He ___ with his new girlfriend.'
   a hung out   **c** has been hanging out
   b hangs out   **d** has hung out

4 'Didn't Jenny and Clare fall out last week?'
  'Yes, but they ___ now.'
   a were making up
   b have been making up
   c made up
   d have made up

5 '___ the invitations to the party out yet?'
  'Yes, I did it last week.'
   a Has she sent
   b Have you been sending
   c Are you sending
   d Have you sent

6 Call me ___ your mum gets home. I need to speak to her immediately!
   a by the time   **c** the moment
   b until   **d** before

7 ___ I've finished my homework, it'll be midnight.
   a As soon as   **c** Before
   b By the time   **d** When

8 The Mediterranean, ___ this species of fish is found, is becoming more and more polluted.
   a whose   **c** where
   b when   **d** which

9 London, ___ is the capital of England, used to be much dirtier than it is now.
   a where   **c** who
   b which   **d** that

10 Scientists are studying this rare species, ___ natural habitat is the bottom of the ocean.
   a where   **c** whose
   b which   **d** who

11 It seems that we ___ destroying the rainforests until it is too late.
   a aren't stopping   **c** will stop
   b don't stop   **d** won't stop

12 ___ Great White Shark is an endangered species.
   a -   **c** The
   b A   **d** An

13 In a big city like New York, ___ Jodie lives, it isn't easy to meet people.
   a where   **c** that
   b which   **d** when

14 There's ___ article in the paper today about the gorillas in the Congo.
   a a   **c** the
   b an   **d** -

15 Humans ___ the planet for centuries.
   a have been damaging
   b have damaging
   c has damaged
   d have been damaged

16 ___ Mount Everest is in Nepal.
   a -   **c** An
   b The   **d** A

17 Grant ___ to the library. He should be back soon.
   a has been going   **c** is going
   b has gone   **d** has going

18 Is that the place ___ you met your girlfriend?
   a who   **c** whose
   b which   **d** where

Reading

A Read the *Exam Reminder*. When can you eliminate an answer option?

_____

B Now complete the *Exam Task*.

1

Hi Ralph!

Well, it's 36°C here in Bordeaux and I am having a great time! I'm staying in the historical part of the city and I've already fallen in love with the area! I'm sleeping in a tent, though, so I just hope there won't be any storms while I'm here ...

Ben

2

Hi Tim,

Thanks for waiting for the cleaner to come. Remember your keys and please lock the door when you leave.

Dad

3

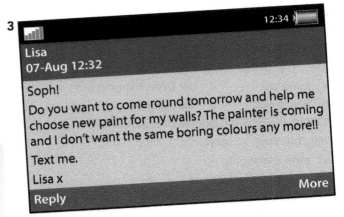

12:34

Lisa
07-Aug 12:32

Soph!
Do you want to come round tomorrow and help me choose new paint for my walls? The painter is coming and I don't want the same boring colours any more!!

Text me.

Lisa x

Reply   More

4

Top Tips for Ed's Electricians
1 Arrive for each job on time.
2 Remain polite at all times.
3 Apologise to your customer if there are any problems.

5

Urgent

Great party last night!
Loads of damage to the flat, though. Let's get together to discuss how we can tidy it up.

Midday in the lounge.

Thanks, Quentin

Exam Task

Look at each of the texts. What do they say? Choose the correct letter **a**, **b** or **c**.

1 What does Ben hope?
- **a** that the weather doesn't change
- **b** that he will like the area
- **c** that he will sleep in a tent

2 Why has Tim's dad written the note?
- **a** to remind him to take his keys
- **b** to remind him the cleaner is coming
- **c** to remind him the door is locked

3 What should Soph do?
- **a** get in touch with Lisa   **b** paint Lisa's walls   **c** find a painter

4 What should Ed's Electricians do?
- **a** arrive early
- **b** create problems with their customers
- **c** say 'sorry' if they create an inconvenience

5 What must Quentin's flatmates do?
- **a** clean the flat straight away
- **b** meet to consider how to clean the flat up
- **c** have a party

Vocabulary

A Choose the correct answers.

1 Please clean the ___. I can't see the garden.
 a windows b wall c sink

2 Will you put the dirty dishes in the ___?
 a fridge b sink c toilets

3 His flat is on the 3rd ___.
 a ground b floor c lift

4 Look in the ___ if you're thirsty. I think there's some orange juice.
 a sink b fridge c sofa

5 Jenny has lost the ___ to her house and now she can't get in!
 a wall b door c keys

6 I'm going to sit outside in the ___ today.
 a garden b bed c garage

B Complete the text with these words.

block of flats bungalow castle cottage detached house semi-detached house tent

Find a property

Mandy is an estate agent. It's her job to sell property for other people.

'There are all sorts of properties for sale. Most people in cities prefer to live in a **(1)** _____ even though it can be noisy and sometimes the lifts don't work! As you move away from the city centre and into the suburbs, you'll find that a **(2)** _____ is a good choice; it's not too big and only has one floor, so it's cheaper than a **(3)** _____ which has two floors, is much bigger and is surrounded by its own garden. If you don't mind sharing a wall with a neighbour, you could live in a **(4)** _____.

'Things are different in the countryside. There you can get a pretty little **(5)** _____ or, if you're a millionaire, a big **(6)** _____ fit for a king, or queen of course! The only thing I haven't sold is a **(7)** _____! You can just go to a camping shop for one of those!'

Grammar

will; be going to

A Complete the sentences with the tenses and verbs in brackets.

1 Jim _____ me to the shop. (**be going to / not drive**)

2 _____ you _____ the bathroom, please? (**future simple / clean**)

3 Be careful! You _____ that window. (**be going to / break**)

4 The decorators _____ the house on Sunday. (**be going to / paint**)

5 I promise I _____ my bedroom before my mum gets home. (**future simple / tidy**)

6 Don't worry. I _____ you carry those bags into the kitchen. (**future simple / help**)

7 Our plans have changed. We _____ away this weekend. (**be going to / not go**)

8 Dad _____ my mobile phone bill if I don't do any housework. (**future simple / not pay**)

B Match the first parts of the sentences 1–8 to the second parts a–h.

1 I will buy my own house ☐
2 I'm going to paint my room ☐
3 Next week I'm going to ☐
4 She'll ☐
5 I'll cook dinner ☐
6 Will you please ☐
7 Walk the dog ☐
8 Martha is going to have ☐

a and Mum can relax.
b go on holiday.
c be 18 in November.
d when I have enough money.
e or you won't get any pocket money!
f in a bright colour.
g a baby in a few months.
h be quiet as I'm trying to work?

Listening

A Read the *Exam Reminder*. What can help you understand technical words?

_____

B 🔊 **5.1** ▷❚❙ Listen and complete the *Exam Task*.

Exam Task

You will hear part of an interview with a lady called Julia who is decorating her house. For questions **1–6**, circle the best answer, **a**, **b** or **c**.

1 Julia is making her home look like a
   a medieval castle.
   b detached house.
   c medieval bungalow.

2 Where does Julia start the visit?
   a on the 3rd floor
   b on the ground floor
   c in the kitchen

3 They need a(n)
   a electrician.
   b painter.
   c plumber.

4 Why is Julia making her house look like one from the Middle Ages?
   a She likes wearing the traditional clothes from the period.
   b She discovered interesting films about the period.
   c She likes romantic people.

5 Julia is worried about changing the garden because
   a it costs a lot of money.
   b the council has not given them permission.
   c the neighbours aren't pleased with the plans.

6 What does Julia say about her future?
   a She will possibly move if the council says no.
   b She will talk to the council.
   c She will probably still change the garden.

C 🔊 **5.1** ▷❚❙ Listen again and check your answers.

Vocabulary

A Complete the collocations with *make, move, do* or *take*.

1 _____ with the times
2 _____ a mess
3 _____ the housework
4 _____ house
5 _____ a break
6 _____ a bath
7 _____ your bed
8 _____ the dishes

B Circle the correct words.

1 I must do house / the housework. The house is in a mess!

2 We are moving with the times / house next year. We've bought a little cottage.

3 You should make a mess / your bed the moment you get up.

4 Call me at ten. I'll be taking a break / a bath then.

5 Please don't make your bed / a mess. I've just cleaned up in here.

6 Let's do a break / the dishes before we go to bed.

7 Penny's so old-fashioned. She needs to move with the times / house.

8 I'll take a bath / the dishes after the football game.

Grammar

Future Plans and Events; Future Predictions

A Correct the sentences.

1 Oh no! The crystal vase is going fall over.
2 Don't worry. I'll doing the dishes later.
3 The train leave at 6pm on Saturday.
4 They be moving to a cottage next month.
5 Do the job properly or I won't to pay you.
6 Samantha might to spend all of her money before the house is finished.

B Complete the text by writing one word in each gap.

A footballer's life

Meet Blaine Goonie. He's a football player with Munchuster United. Next week, he **(1)** _____ travelling to Spain to play in a very important Champions League match. Unfortunately for Blaine, the experts predict Real Madrid **(2)** _____ probably **(3)** _____ the winners on Saturday night.

Blaine makes a lot of money and he knows how to spend it! He had an expensive wedding last month and now he and his new wife, Jolene, are **(4)** _____ to buy a castle in the English countryside! They **(5)** _____ getting a famous Italian interior designer to decorate it and, when the castle is ready, a celebrity magazine **(6)** _____ visit them to take photos of it, I think. Blaine and Jolene love the attention! They have been famous for a long time, but they never get tired of it!

Use your English

A Complete the second sentences so that they have a similar meaning to the first sentences, using the words in bold. Use between two and five words.

1 It's my 18th birthday tomorrow!
   be
   I _____ 18 tomorrow!

2 Let's not do the gardening. Look at those dark clouds.
   going
   Let's not do the gardening. I think _____ rain.

3 Jack has plans to buy a sofa for his new house next week.
   is
   Jack _____ a sofa for his new house next week.

4 I'm sorry, Dad. It was wrong of me to come home so late.
   won't
   I'm sorry, Dad. I promise _____ so late again.

5 I'll make my decision about the flat tomorrow.
   am
   I _____ the flat tomorrow.

writing: an informal letter

A **Complete the sentences with these words.**

can't   fantastic   I'll   of course   really

1 Apologising: I'm _____ sorry.
2 Expressing enthusiasm: Congratulations! What _____ news!
3 Giving information: _____ be at the station at two o'clock.
4 Accepting an invitation: _____ I'll be there!
5 Rejecting an invitation: Unfortunately, I _____ make it …

B **Read the writing task below and then circle the correct words in the sentences.**

You have received a letter from your cousin, Cathy, who is moving to another city to start university. Write a letter in reply to Cathy.

Hi Julie,

How are you? You'll never guess where I am! I'm in Edinburgh, Scotland. I got a place at the university here and I'm really excited!

My course starts in three weeks and I'm here looking for a flat to rent. Everything is pretty expensive, but I think I'll be OK if I can get some cheap furniture. Can you help me? Is there anything you don't need at your house?

When the flat is ready, I'd like you to come and stay for a weekend. I'd love to see you, and we'll have a great time in Edinburgh. It's very pretty and the people are lovely.

Let me know when you can come. You can take the train from Manchester and I'll pick you up at the station in my car.

Bye for now,

Cathy

1 Cathy is in Edinburgh now to find a place to stay / start her university course.
2 Cathy wants Julie to give her some money for a deposit / any old furniture she doesn't need.
3 Cathy has invited Julie to a party / to spend a few days with her.
4 Julie can travel to Edinburgh by train / car.

C **Read the example letter and answer the questions.**

Hi Cathy,

Congratulations! What fantastic news! I've heard that Scotland is amazing and everyone says that Edinburgh is beautiful. You're so lucky!

I hope you find a place soon and yes, I can help you. I've got a desk and a chair you can have. They're old, but in good condition. I've also got a nice big red leather sofa, if you want it, too.

Of course I'll visit you! I'd love to see your new place and spend some time in Edinburgh. I'm really looking forward to it!

The best time for me to come is the end of October as I've got some free time then. In fact, I can come on Friday 28th and leave on Monday morning. Is that OK?

See you soon,

Julie

1 Has Julie responded to all of Cathy's letter?
2 Has Julie replied to Cathy's questions in the same order as Cathy asked them?
3 Has Julie written in a formal or an informal style?

D **Read and complete the *Exam Task* below. Don't forget to use the *Useful Expressions* on page 67 of your Student's Book.**

Exam Task

Write a **letter** in reply to Cathy using these notes. (100 words)

- congratulate Cathy on her good news
- tell her you can give her a fridge and a bed
- accept her invitation
- tell her you can visit at the end of November

Reading

A **Read the *Exam Reminder*. Do you need to match all of the texts to a description?**

_____

B **Now complete the *Exam Task*.**

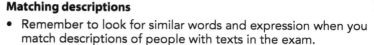

Matching descriptions

- Remember to look for similar words and expression when you match descriptions of people with texts in the exam.
- Underline the key words in the description of the first person.
- Next, look for words and expressions in the texts that are similar to the words you underlined.
- Do the same for each description.
- Finally, check the answers carefully. There will be three of the longer texts that you won't match to a description.

a **Tom's Trekking** is ideal for nature lovers. You can walk along mountain and forest paths with professional guides throughout the year, on either a one-day trek or three-day trek which includes staying in tents overnight. You must be in good physical condition. Ages 10–65 are welcome, but children must be accompanied by an adult.

b With **Mountain Rafting Adventures**, you can travel down fast-flowing rivers in inflatable boats and jump into the water when you arrive at the finish. You must be able to swim. A life jacket, helmet and paddle will be provided.

c **Rod's Rock Climbing Tours** offers climbing throughout the year, taught by professional instructors. You should not suffer from a fear of heights, and should have good coordination. Fifty pounds for a weekend; discounts for groups of four or more!

d Tour mountain trails with **Just Biking**. You must have your own mountain bike and helmet. Monthly competitions. Call Mike on (020) 8510 1123.

e **Ellie's Environment** provides a fantastic camping experience whilst also caring for the environment. Listen to the sounds of nature by sleeping under the trees or in your own tent, and go to classes to learn how to help keep our planet beautiful.

f **Climbing in the Trees** is fun for all of the family and even for those who don't like heights! You don't have to reach the top; from the ground to the treetops we have plenty of areas to reach, which are all at different levels.

g Visit this **coastal castle**, one of the main tourist attractions of the area. Visitors can enjoy learning all about the history of this beautiful castle, as well as having beautiful views over the sea.

h In this **historic house**, which used to belong to royalty, you can visit the kitchens and see the bedrooms, as well as walk through the gardens and see where the family used to go swimming in their own pool.

Exam Task

The teenagers below are all looking for an activity to do. There are descriptions of eight activities for young people. Decide which activity would be the most suitable for the following teenagers. For questions 1–5, mark the correct letter **a–h**.

1 Julie is happiest when she is outdoors and is very interested in working in the eco-tourism industry when she's older. ☐

2 Maxence wants to do something with his older brother. He is afraid of high places but really enjoys being active outdoors. ☐

3 Aurélie thinks it will be hot at the weekend and so wants to go up to the mountains where it will be cooler. She wants to be able to go swimming there. ☐

4 Thom is 12 years old and has always loved cycling. He is very competitive, has his own equipment and wants to try his favourite activity in a new area. ☐

5 Lise loves camping and would like to camp overnight on a busy activity in the countryside lasting at least two days. ☐

Vocabulary

A Circle the correct words.

1 When you play tennis, you hit the ball with a bat / **racket** / stick.
2 You need a net to play aerobics / judo / **volleyball**.
3 Cyclists should always wear a cap / glove / **helmet** to protect their head.
4 I got bored watching the runners on the pitch / pool / **track**.
5 Volleyball is one of the most popular individual / professional / **team** sports at the Olympics.
6 He prefers **individual** / team / indoor sports like weightlifting and cycling.
7 The football fans went crazy when the umpire / line judge / **referee** showed a player the red card.
8 He wanted to go weightlifting / swimming / **skiing** last week, but there was no snow.

B Match the first parts of the sentences 1–6 to the second parts a–f.

1 Joe competed ☐   **a** Sally, but she's much better at tennis.
2 If you want to succeed ☐   **b** this game, we'll win the whole tournament!
3 Helen would like to beat ☐   **c** because he wasn't wearing a helmet.
4 I didn't agree with the umpire's ☐   **d** in swimming, you need strong arms.
5 If we win ☐   **e** decision in the last game of tennis.
6 John hurt his head ☐   **f** in the tournament and came second.

Grammar

Conditionals: Zero & First

A Circle the correct words.

1 If she sat / **sits** on the beach, she gets sunburnt.
2 Tom **will play** / plays tennis if he finds his racket.
3 If Roger **can** / could swim, we'll go in the sea.
4 We **will go** / go running tomorrow if we aren't tired.
5 Harry shouts a lot when he watched / **watches** a football game.
6 If Alicia goes to the game, I **will go** / went, too.

B Complete the text with these words.

become   don't   eat   have   stop   take   will   won't

Calorie maths!

If you (**1**) _____ exercise and eat more than you should, you will (**2**) _____ overweight. It's that simple. In fact, it's basic mathematics – if you (**3**) _____ in more calories than you burn, you (**4**) _____ store fat. The average 13-year-old girl needs approximately 2,000 calories a day to stay healthy, while for boys the figure is 2,200 calories. Now, that doesn't mean you can eat 2,000 calories of junk food. Compare, for example, a small bar of chocolate and a plate of chicken and vegetables. If you (**5**) _____ the chocolate, you (**6**) _____ get any vitamins or protein, and it won't (**7**) _____ you from feeling hungry. The chocolate contains 600 calories, whereas the chicken dish has just 450. So, if you choose the chocolate, you will be hungry and gain weight! However, if you eat just a little of it and do some form of exercise regularly, you won't (**8**) _____ any problems.

Listening

A Read the *Exam Reminder*. When is it important to identify emotions in pictures?

_____

B 6.1 ▶️📶 Listen and complete the *Exam Task*.

Exam Task

There are six questions in this part. For each question, there are three pictures and a short recording. Circle the correct answer **a**, **b** or **c**.

1 Which injury does Wayne Rooney have?

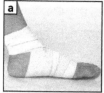  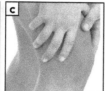

2 What do the speakers think of the Six Nations?

3 Which country is likely to win the Six Nations?

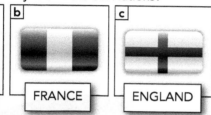

4 Which type of weather has cancelled the football?

  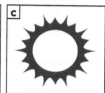

5 What does Venus Williams have her own label of?

6 What do Australian children often do after school?

C 6.1 ▶️📶 Listen again and check your answers.

Vocabulary

A Complete the text with the correct form of these words.

> compete   definite   follow   proper

The beautiful game

When it comes to sport, there's (1) _____ no bigger event than the football World Cup. Billions of people around the world support their teams as they (2) _____ for the trophy. The players dream of victory, while the fans wait for the match to begin!

In its long history, there have been many memorable moments. Who could forget the 1986 cup, when (3) _____ of football watched Diego Maradona score a goal that is remembered as one of the most controversial of all time? Fans said it wasn't a (4) _____ goal because it looked as if he touched the ball with his hand before he scored, which is not allowed.

B Complete the sentences with the correct form of the words.

1 Skiing can be _____ if you don't get lessons.
2 What is the _____ of the water in this swimming pool?
3 Bungee jumping can be very dangerous if it's not done _____.
4 Young children shouldn't go swimming without _____.
5 The game of chess requires a lot of _____.
6 Are you _____ on Sunday? I want to go cycling.

DANGER

DEEP

PROPER

SUPERVISE

CONCENTRATE

FREE

Ready, Steady, Go! **6**   35

Grammar

Second Conditional

A Complete the dialogues with the correct form of the verbs in brackets.

1 **A:** I'm worried that I'm a bit overweight.
  B: You _____ (be) slimmer if you _____ (do) more exercise.

2 **A:** John's always thirsty after school.
  B: If he _____ (drink) more water in the lunch break, he _____ (not feel) so thirsty.

3 **A:** What _____ (you / do) if you _____ (disagree) with the umpire?
  B: I probably wouldn't say anything until after the match.

4 **A:** If I _____ (have) the time, I _____ (join) the mountain climbing group.
  B: Yes, I think you would really like it.

B Rewrite as Second Conditional sentences.

1 You need a tennis racket. I don't have one to give you.
  If _____ it to you.

2 I won't have time. I can't go to the match.
  If _____ to the match.

3 The teenagers don't have tickets, so they can't watch the game.
  If _____ the game.

4 I don't have a pen, so I can't write down the score.
  I _____ a pen.

5 Liz wants to do aerobics. She hasn't got the time.
  Liz _____ the time.

6 They don't have the money. They won't go snowboarding.
  They _____ the money.

Use your English

A Complete the text with the correct form of the words.

Dying to play

If I (1) _____ you that they killed the captain of the losing team in Mayan football, (2) _____ you believe me? It's true! For the Maya, it was considered an honour to lose their (3) _____ and be sacrificed to the gods!

This (4) _____ game was invented over 3,000 years ago. It (5) _____ a combination of basketball and football and was an (6) _____ game. The ball was not allowed to touch the ground. The (7) _____ bounced it off the walls with their elbows, hips, knees or head, but using their hands was against the rules, just as it is in football. To score a point, the (8) _____ had to get the ball through a stone hoop, in a similar way to basketball.

It required a lot of (9) _____ and was not a game for children. As it was a very quick game, the players had to be (10) _____. They also had to show great courage and (11) _____ in their abilities; after all, one of them would die if they (12) _____.

TELL

WILL

FREE
DANGER
BE
OUT

PLAY

COMPETE

CONCENTRATE

ATHLETE
CONFIDENT

LOSE

Writing: sentence transformation (1)

A **Circle the correct words.**

1 He wanted to stay at home in order to / so that watch the basketball match.

2 Will you come with me to the park so as / to help me find my cycling helmet?

3 The referee gave him a warning because / for he was fighting.

4 She joined the team so that / because she could improve her skills.

5 I like cycling so / for the freedom and independence it gives me.

B **Read the writing task below and then answer the questions about it.**

Here are some questions about outdoor activities. For each question 1–5, complete the second sentence so that it means the same as the first. Use no more than three words.

1 Are the sentences about different topics? _____

2 How many questions are there? _____

3 How many words do you use? _____

4 Do you complete the first sentence or the second sentence? _____

C **Read the example task and circle the correct words.**

1 I won the tennis tournament last year.
   I have been the tennis champion for / since one year.

2 He wanted to be the referee's assistant.
   He wanted to assisted / assist the referee.

D **Read and complete the *Exam Task* below.**

Exam Task

Here are some sentences about outdoor activities. For each question **1–5**, complete the second sentence so that it means the same as the first. **Use no more than three words.**

1 She said nice things about my karate skills.
   She complimented _____ on my karate skills.

2 I think this is Sarah's racket.
   I think this racket belongs _____.

3 If you don't make your bed, you can't go swimming.
   Unless _____ your bed, you can't go swimming.

4 Many people admire sporting heroes such as Usain Bolt.
   Many people look _____ sporting heroes such as Usain Bolt.

5 I stopped taking tennis lessons five years ago.
   I _____ tennis lessons for five years.

Learning Reminder

Clauses of purpose

Remember to use these clauses of purpose to explain why something happens or why someone does something:

- *because* + subject + verb, e.g. *He wore a helmet because he wanted to be safe.*
- *so as to* + infinitive, e.g. *He wore a helmet so as to be safe.*
- *for* + noun, e.g. *He wore a helmet for safety.*
- infinitive, e.g. *He wore a helmet to be safe.*
- *so that* + subject + verb, e.g. *He wore a helmet so that he could be safe.*
- *in order to* + infinitive, e.g. *He wore a helmet in order to be safe.*

Vocabulary

A Choose the correct answers.

1 She is moving to a ___ of flats near the city centre.
- **a** block
- **b** ground
- **c** floor
- **d** lift

2 I don't want to live in the city any more. I'd like to live in a nice ___ in the country.
- **a** tent
- **b** block of flats
- **c** garage
- **d** cottage

3 There is a big ___ around the house, so that nobody can see into the garden.
- **a** wall
- **b** door
- **c** floor
- **d** garage

4 After the earthquake, people camped in ___ for weeks.
- **a** bungalows
- **b** castles
- **c** tents
- **d** cottages

5 The landlord will give us our ___ the day before we move in.
- **a** lift
- **b** ground floor
- **c** keys
- **d** door

6 Sarah is tired from cleaning the kitchen so she is going to ___ a break.
- **a** move
- **b** make
- **c** take
- **d** do

7 Most people hate doing ___, but I find it relaxing.
- **a** house
- **b** a break
- **c** their bed
- **d** housework

8 He has ___ such a mess in the kitchen! It's going to take hours to clean.
- **a** did
- **b** moved
- **c** made
- **d** took

9 They have packed everything in boxes because they are ___ house.
- **a** having
- **b** leaving
- **c** moving
- **d** making

10 In this race, the competitors run seven times around the ___.
- **a** track
- **b** pool
- **c** pitch
- **d** goal post

11 The tennis player threw his ___ to the floor when he lost the match.
- **a** bat
- **b** racket
- **c** glove
- **d** stick

12 There is water under the kitchen sink, so I'm going to call the ___.
- **a** plumber
- **b** cleaner
- **c** painter
- **d** electrician

13 The karate ___ said that I've improved a lot this year.
- **a** competitor
- **b** instructor
- **c** umpire
- **d** athlete

14 The ___ sent the footballer off the pitch for behaving badly.
- **a** line judge
- **b** referee
- **c** umpire
- **d** supervisor

15 'Why are you training so hard?'
'Because I'm going to ___ in the Olympic Games.'
- **a** supervise
- **b** succeed
- **c** compete
- **d** concentrate

16 Your flat is really dirty! Why don't you hire a ___?
- **a** builder
- **b** painter
- **c** plumber
- **d** cleaner

17 He nearly scored a goal yesterday, but the ball hit the goal ___.
- **a** pool
- **b** basket
- **c** post
- **d** stick

18 We play volleyball just for the ___; we don't want to enter any tournaments.
- **a** enjoyment
- **b** competition
- **c** supervision
- **d** concentration

19 How ___ did you go when you tried scuba diving?
- **a** depth
- **b** deepen
- **c** deeply
- **d** deep

20 I like trying new sports because I like to have a ___.
- **a** confidence
- **b** challenge
- **c** competition
- **d** supervisor

Grammar

B Choose the correct answers.

1   Next week, I hope we ___ in the championship match.
   a   will play   c   play
   b   will playing   d   would play

2   'So, Mike, do you think your team will beat Manchester United?'
   'Yes, we are the best team and we ___.'
   a   are going to win   c   win
   b   are winning   d   would win

3   If they ___ an extension, their house would be bigger.
   a   built   c   would build
   b   will build   d   build

4   'What time are you coming to watch the match on TV?'
   'It ___ at eight, so I'll be there a little earlier.'
   a   has started   c   starts
   b   would start   d   started

5   If she ___, her fans will celebrate in the streets.
   a   won   c   will win
   b   wins   d   had won

6   Who do you believe ___ be first over the finishing line?
   a   is going   c   would
   b   will   d   is

7   'What would you do if you won some money?'
   'I think ___ the house, because it's really old-fashioned.'
   a   I'd decorate   c   I'm decorating
   b   I'll decorate   d   I decorated

8   ___ the living room this afternoon, please?
   a   Are you tidying   c   Do you tidy
   b   Will you tidy   d   Won't you tidy

9   We ___ house if the neighbours were noisy.
   a   moved   c   will move
   b   would move   d   won't move

10 We ___ in the final at the weekend if we come first in this race.
   a   competed   c   compete
   b   will compete   d   would compete

11 People ___ in terraced houses in the future.
   a   won't live   c   wouldn't live
   b   would live   d   are living

12 'I've finally decided what to put in the new living room.'
   'Really? What ___ put in there?'
   a   will you
   b   are you going to
   c   you going to
   d   are you

13 'Look! It has started to rain.'
   'Oh, ___ all the windows, please?'
   a   are you going to close
   b   are you closing
   c   will you close
   d   won't you close

14 If it snows later, we ___ snowboarding.
   a   go   c   is going to go
   b   will go   d   would go

15 I ___ fitter if I took up jogging.
   a   wouldn't be
   b   am going to be
   c   would be
   d   will be

16 'Ann, we're going to Grandma's house tomorrow.'
   'I can't come, I ___ tennis.'
   a   play   c   will play
   b   am playing   d   played

17 If it's hot, I always ___ a cap.
   a   would wear   c   wear
   b   will wear   d   am wearing

18 Don't forget! The train ___ at six o'clock.
   a   would leave   c   leaves
   b   will leave   d   leave

Reading

A Read the *Exam Reminder*. Why should you make notes about each paragraph?

_____

B Now complete the *Exam Task*.

Lost in the mountains

Josh Linden, 16, had a scary experience last year. During a camping trip with his family, he got lost on a mountain peak. This is Josh's story of his ordeal and how he coped with it.

Autumn in the mountains is a beautiful time; the changing colours of the leaves on the trees, the beautiful mountain peaks and valleys and the chance to be outdoors attract thousands of campers, including my family. We'd been camping regularly since I was seven, and I thought I was an experienced hiker with good survival skills.

Last year was no different. We had been planning our yearly camping trip for months. We were going to spend five days hiking and camping in the mountains in the north of the country. The landscape was really beautiful, the sun shone brightly and we spent every day hiking in the mountains and then camping at night.

On the last day, we set out for a final hike. After reaching the end of a long trail, we put up the tents to camp there for the night. However, I'm an impatient person and it was still daylight, so I decided to explore the area a bit on my own. My dad warned me not to go too far away and told me that I should keep the sun behind me and to the left so that I could find the camp again.

Unfortunately, I wasn't listening to Dad. I'd heard from other campers that there were deer in the area and I wanted to see them. All I took with me was my camera. I was searching for the deer for about 30 minutes when I saw some animal tracks on the ground. I was sure they were from a deer, so I followed them. I went deeper into the forest, but I wasn't worried – I was certain I could find my way back to camp. All of a sudden, there they were – a herd of deer, around ten of them. I couldn't believe my luck! I watched them for a while and then started taking photos. As I tried to get closer, I made a sound, and the deer turned and ran away. I should have stayed where I was, but stupidly, I followed them. I could hear them in the distance ahead of me and I kept running towards the sound, crashing into trees as I ran, but they knew where to hide. After a while, I was exhausted and decided it was time to go back to camp. Suddenly, I realised that the sun had gone down and it was now evening. I realised with a shock that I wouldn't be able to get my directions by looking at the sun and I had no idea where I was. I was exhausted. I began to feel panic and started shouting for help, but no one heard me. Basically, I had two choices; I could look for the camp in darkness, or I could spend the night alone on the mountain and find the camp when the sun came up. Choosing the second option, I broke branches off a tree to make a bed that would keep me off the cold ground. I was hungry and thirsty, but there was nothing I could do about it. What a cold, miserable night I spent on that mountain alone.

The next morning, I noted the position of the sun and began walking quickly, trying to find something that looked familiar. Before long, I thought I heard shouting. I stopped moving and listened carefully. Yes! It was my dad calling my name. I shouted back and he soon found me. I can't tell you how glad I was to see him! My dad was glad to see me, too, but that didn't stop him from telling me what an absolute idiot I'd been!

Exam Task

Read the text and questions below. For each question, choose the correct letter **a**, **b**, **c** or **d**.

1 What is Josh doing in the text?
- **a** describing a film he saw
- **b** persuading others to organise their own camping holidays
- **c** giving advice on what to do on camping holidays
- **d** explaining what happened on a trip he went on

2 Why did Josh get lost?
- **a** He didn't listen to advice.
- **b** He didn't hear the other campers.
- **c** No one saved him
- **d** The sun was too bright.

3 How did Josh feel when he realised he was lost?
- **a** very silly
- **b** very hungry
- **c** frightened
- **d** a bit thirsty

4 How did Josh survive?
- **a** by following the deer
- **b** by protecting his body from the cold
- **c** by looking for familiar places
- **d** by finding food to eat

5 What is the reading text mainly about?
- **a** how easily you can survive a night in the forest
- **b** how easily you can get into trouble in the outdoors
- **c** how long you need to become an experienced camper
- **d** how to look for deer in the forest

Vocabulary

A Complete the text with the correct form of these words.

cope   die   disappear   give   injure   survive

Left for dead

Joe Simpson and Simon Yates were climbing down a mountain in the Andes when Simpson slipped and (1) _____ his leg. Then, while Yates was trying to lower him down the mountain on the end of a rope, Simpson went over a cliff and totally (2) _____. Yates couldn't see or hear him, but he held on tightly hoping that Simpson was still alive.

After some time, believing that Simpson had (3) _____, Yates cut the rope and climbed down the mountain. When the rope was cut, Simpson, who was actually still alive, fell down to the bottom of the mountain. He then spent three days without food or water moving slowly across rocky ground towards the camp. He never (4) _____ up.

Incredibly, in the middle of the night, he arrived at the camp. Luckily, Yates found him. Later, Simpson wrote a book about how he (5) _____ on his own, and how he (6) _____ with the terrible thirst, hunger and pain.

B Complete the words in the sentences.

1 Your d _ _ _ _ _ _ _ _ _ is the place where your trip ends.
2 An e _ _ _ _ _ _ _ is someone who goes to places not many people have been to.
3 An e _ _ _ _ _ _ _ _ _ is a trip to see something very far away.
4 A j _ _ _ _ _ _ is another name for a trip.
5 The c _ _ _ _ _ _ _ _ _ are your circumstances or the way things are around you.
6 The person you travel or live with is called your c _ _ _ _ _ _ _ _.

Grammar

Past Perfect Simple; Past Perfect Continuous

A Circle the correct words.

1 Poor Steve had been walking / had walked around the forest for hours before the rescue team found him.
2 Until she graduated, Maxine had never visited / never visited a foreign country.
3 The moment we had seen / saw the crocodiles, we knew we were in trouble.
4 Carrie had already reached / had already been reaching the top when the other climbers got there.
5 The divers had checked their equipment before they had entered / entered the water.
6 She had been walking next to the river when she heard / had heard a strange noise.
7 Angelina got to the mountain, had picked up / picked up the map and started walking.

B Complete the second sentences so that they have a similar meaning to the first sentences. Use the words in bold.

1 Simon started walking at six o'clock. **walking**
   By nine o'clock, Simon _____ for three hours.
2 Susan ran and she got tired. **been**
   Susan got tired because _____.
3 They had lunch at one o'clock. The trip began at two o'clock. **before**
   They _____ the trip began.
4 First, Jill packed her bag. Then she rang for a taxi. **had**
   Jill _____ before she rang for a taxi.
5 Natasha got to the river 20 minutes before us. **waiting**
   Natasha _____ for 20 minutes at the river before we got there.

Listening

A Read the *Exam Reminder*. What word will you hear if a letter is repeated in a word?

_____

B 🔊 **7.1** Listen and complete the *Exam Task*.

Exam Reminder

Checking spelling

- Don't forget to think about what the missing words might be for each gap.
- Be careful – you need to spell the words correctly to get a correct answer.
- Remember that you will hear the word 'double' if there is a repeated letter in a word.

Exam Task

You will hear some information about a famous explorer. For each question, fill in the missing information in the numbered space.

The famous explorer

Name: Robert (**1**) _____

Number of deep-sea journeys: (**2**) _____

First childhood hero: (**3**) _____

First expedition: when he was still at (**4**) _____

Nowadays: still an (**5**) _____

His favourite place: (**6**) _____

C 🔊 **7.1** Listen again and check your answers.

Vocabulary

A Circle the correct words.

1 Deserts run across / through much of central Australia.
2 Across / Over the years, we have learnt a lot about extreme weather.
3 This mountain is about / between the same size as the one I climbed last year.
4 In summer, the temperature here can be up / over 45° Celsius.
5 In Antarctica, the temperature is often below / under freezing.
6 The driest place in / on the planet is the Atacama Desert in Chile.
7 While the surfer was in / at the water, he saw a huge shark in the distance.
8 The city of La Paz in Bolivia is located 3,660 metres above / over sea level.

B Complete the sentences with the correct form of these words.

do   get   go   go   keep   save

1 I didn't take a map with me and I _____ lost.
2 We _____ on a journey across the mountains.
3 Samantha's quick thinking _____ the climber's life.
4 'Just _____ calm,' said Josh when our boat sank.
5 An explorer has _____ missing in the Amazon jungle.
6 Just _____ your best and everything will be fine.

Grammar

Question Tags; Subject & Object Questions

A Circle the correct words.

1 You don't really want to do that, do / **don't** you?
2 We couldn't stop it, could / **couldn't** we?
3 You'll tell me if you see him, don't / **won't** you?
4 The food's bad, **isn't** / wasn't it?
5 You won't be angry, are / **will** you?
6 You wanted that map, won't / **didn't** you?

B Read the text and then write the questions by looking at the answers.

Lord of the Flies

William Golding's novel *Lord of the Flies* is a story about a group of young British schoolboys who are stranded on a tropical island after their plane crashes on its way to England. Two of the boys, Ralph and Piggy, find a shell in the water and use it to call all the other survivors. Ralph becomes the boys' leader. Using Piggy's glasses, they light a fire on the top of a mountain to get the attention of passing ships. For a while, they work together as a team, but soon their good behaviour turns into bad behaviour, when, led by a boy named Jack, they turn to violence and murder. When they are finally rescued by an officer from a ship, they realise what they have done.

1 _____
William Golding.

2 _____
They find a shell.

3 _____
They use Piggy's glasses.

4 _____
An officer.

Use your English

A Choose the correct answers.

Swimming the Atlantic

Who (**1**) ___ the first person to swim across the Atlantic Ocean? It was 31-year-old Frenchman, Benoît Lecomte, a long-distance swimmer. After swimming nearly 6,000 kilometres (**2**) ___ the Atlantic Ocean, his first words were, 'Never again!'

Lecomte (**3**) ___ trained for six years beforehand and he wanted to raise money for cancer research. He set out from Massachusetts on July 16, 1998 and (**4**) ___ for 73 days when he finally arrived at Quiberon, in north west France. Lecomte stopped at the Azores (**5**) ___ the middle of the Atlantic because he was exhausted. He stayed there for a week to (**6**) ___ and then completed his amazing swim.

The human body could not survive 24 hours a day for 73 days (**7**) ___ the North Atlantic Ocean. That's why Benoît swam for six to eight hours a day. He swam beside his support boat and had to eat 9,000 calories a day. He faced sharks, six-metre-high waves and storms. (**8**) ___ that an incredible achievement?

1	**a** had been	**b** was	**c** he was	**d** was being
2	**a** across	**b** over	**c** above	**d** through
3	**a** was	**b** has	**c** had	**d** is
4	**a** swam	**b** swims	**c** had swum	**d** had been swimming
5	**a** in	**b** from	**c** under	**d** over
6	**a** get on	**b** get lost	**c** get better	**d** do his best
7	**a** on	**b** in	**c** at	**d** with
8	**a** Wasn't	**b** Don't	**c** Can't	**d** Hasn't

writing: a story (2)

A Complete the gaps with *Past Simple, Past Continuous, Past Perfect Simple* or *Past Perfect Continuous.*

1 When you want to talk about an action that started and finished in the past, or several actions that happened one after the other in the past, use the

_____.

2 You can talk about an action that was in progress for some time in the past and was interrupted by another past action, or an action which has an effect on a later event in the past by using the

_____.

3 If you want to talk about an action that happened before the time of the story or before another past action, use the

_____.

4 In order to set the scene of a story, or to talk about an action that was in progress in the past that was interrupted by another action, use the _____.

Narrative tenses

Remember to use narrative tenses when writing a story that takes place in the past. These are the Past Simple, the Past Continuous, the Past Perfect Simple and the Past Perfect Continuous. Make sure you know when to use each of these tenses.

- Use the Past Simple for completed states or actions, a series of actions in the past or to take the action of the story further.
- Use the Past Continuous for setting the scene and for talking about an action in progress in the past when another action interrupted it.
- Use the Past Perfect Simple for talking about actions that happened before another past action or before the time of the narrative.
- Use the Past Perfect Continuous for talking about actions in progress for a long time in the past which were interrupted by another past action, or which affected a later event in the past.

B Read the writing task below and then answer the questions about it.

Your English teacher has asked you to write a story. Your story must begin with this sentence: The teenagers were scared and they had no idea where they were.

1 Is someone lost? _____

2 How are they feeling? _____

3 What will they do? _____

C Read the example story and then put the events in the correct order 1–5.

> Use the sentence you were given and say where the story is set.

> Describe the scene and give more details.

> Introduce the main character and a plan of action.

> Describe how the plan is carried out and what happens next.

The teenagers were scared and they had no idea where they were. All around them there were trees, birds, flowers and several paths. One of those paths led to their camp, but which one was it?

They had been walking through the jungle with the rest of the group when they got lost. They didn't know what to do, so they sat down to rest while they decided.

Sally, one of the teenagers, walked off to to look at some flowers. All of a sudden, she heard a terrifying sound. She quickly hid behind a tree and took a deep breath, then she looked. It was a tiger! She couldn't believe it! How would she escape? She had to think fast. The tiger was drinking water at a nearby stream. If she tried to run, it would hear her. What could she do? 'I know!' thought Sally.

Shaking with fear, she picked up a small rock and threw it. The tiger ran towards the sound and Sally ran the opposite way. She ran as fast as she could and finally she saw the camp. She was safe! Now she just had to go back and get the others.

☐ Sally came up with a plan.
☐ Sally managed to escape.
☐ Sally heard something that scared her.

☐ Sally got lost in the jungle.
☐ Sally hid behind a tree.

D Read and complete the *Exam Task* below. Don't forget to use the *Useful Expressions* on page 93 of your Student's Book.

Exam Task

Your English teacher has asked you to write a story. Your story must begin with this sentence: *Suddenly, they realised they had lost the map!* (100 words)

➲ Writing Reference p. 179 in Student's Book

Reading

A Read the *Exam Reminder*. What should you do before you read the answer options?

_____

B Now complete the *Exam Task*.

Free time for teens

The way teenagers spend their free time changes from generation to generation. Playing sport, going out with friends, going (**1**) ___ the cinema, listening (**2**) ___ music and watching TV – all of these activities continue to be enjoyed by today's teens as they were by their parents. But there are new interests that are taking up much of their time, due to more and more people having tablets and smart phones. Let's look at the statistics. How much time do you spend online? A British research group (**3**) ___ out that the average UK teenager spends an incredible 31 hours a week online – that's nearly 4.5 hours per day! And what does the average British teen do online? The usual things – social networking, watching videos on YouTube, finding out about health and beauty, and reading about celebrities and sports. To their parents, it (**4**) ___ seem like they're just wasting their time. Fortunately, they're also spending three hours a week doing research for school projects and homework.

American teenagers, (**5**) ___ the other hand, spend most of their free time in front of the television. An American study found (**6**) ___ that teenagers spent more time with traditional media such as television and radio than had been expected. In fact, the study found that the amount of television watched by the typical American teenager has increased in the past five years to three hours and 20 minutes a day. (**7**) ___ people thought that the availability of computers and the Internet at home would encourage American teens to reduce their TV viewing time, (**8**) ___ this hasn't happened. Internet time was found to be two hours and 20 minutes a day and most of that time is spent on social networking sites, such as Facebook.

So, UK teens are to be found online while US teens are sitting in front of the TV. What about teenagers from mainland Europe? How do they spend their free time? A study into their habits has shown that when it comes to free time, boys prefer watching TV and (**9**) ___, while girls spend more time studying and surfing the Net.

The results show a generation that is more traditional than some might expect. European teenagers still spend more time watching television than they spend online – 10.3 hours a week, on average, compared to 9.1 hours spent on the Internet. But video games, at 11.7 hours per week, now consume even more time than TV for European teens. It was also discovered that European teens like doing something else while online. Nearly 50% listen to music on their PC, while 45% watch TV online, for example. Understandably, such statistics are causing concern among parents, doctors and teachers around the world. They believe that teenagers (**10**) ___ be more physically active in order to stay strong and healthy, and to be able to cope with the demands of school. A life spent in front of a screen is not the way to health and happiness!

Vocabulary

A Complete the sentences with these words.

ballet   cookery   drama   martial arts   painting   photography   sculpture

1 Bruce knows how to protect himself. He's a _____ expert.
2 Helena loves _____ – she enjoys making figures from wood.
3 Are you using an expensive camera on your _____ course?
4 I enjoy _____, especially countryside scenes, but I sometimes do pictures of people, too.
5 Lenny is going to study _____ because he wants to be an actor.
6 Some people find _____ boring, but I really enjoy trying out new recipes.
7 What I love about _____ is the music and the costumes the dancers wear.

B Circle the correct words.

1 If you want to take up photography / ballet, you should get yourself a good camera.
2 It's my dream to surround / explore Mammoth Cave in the USA.
3 Some spiders use their hearing and sense of smell to capture / crawl their food.
4 Judo and karate are both examples of martial arts / sculpture.
5 I'm a terrible chef; I must take a cooker / cookery class.
6 Helen's baby has just learnt to destroy / crawl this week.

Grammar

Modals & Semi-modals (1)

A Circle the correct words.

1 We could / are able to try the new art gallery on Elm Street if it rains.
2 Jenny can / could be at the gym.
3 Lisa wasn't able to / didn't have to go out because it was raining.
4 I could / can swim when I was only two years old.
5 You may / ought to take up a hobby in your free time.
6 You may / should see the doctor about your headaches, Dad.
7 We're not sure at the moment, but we may / must join the drama club.
8 The children must / might be hungry. They haven't eaten all day.

B Complete the sentences with these words.

can   can't   could be   may   must   ought   shouldn't   was able to

1 He _____ have an art exhibition next spring.
2 Mum _____ at the supermarket, but I'm not sure.
3 If you have a headache, you _____ to take some medicine.
4 Nick _____ show off like that. It's really annoying.
5 My dad _____ speak German, French and Italian.
6 Carly is only five. She _____ look after herself.
7 I _____ finish my essay last night, thankfully.
8 You _____ be tired. You've been studying all day!

Listening

A Read the *Exam Reminder*. What should you think about before you listen?

_____

B 🔊 8.1 ▶️ **Listen and complete the *Exam Task*.**

Exam Reminder

Predicting from pictures

• Remember to read the questions and look at the pictures before you listen.

• Try to guess what the listening will be about when you look at the pictures.

• Think about the words you might hear for each picture and the differences between the pictures.

Exam Task

There are six questions in this part. For each question, there are three pictures and a short recording. Circle the correct picture **a**, **b** or **c**.

1 What is the woman watching?

  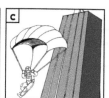

2 How much will the man pay to go canoeing?

 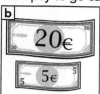 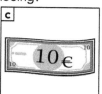

3 Which woman can they see in the picture?

 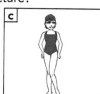

4 Why did he stop horse-riding when he was younger?

5 What did the man eat?

6 When will the girl go on the expedition?

C 🔊 8.1 ▶️ **Listen again and check your answers.**

Vocabulary

A Match the first parts of the sentences 1–5 to the second parts a–e.

1	It's rude to show	☐	**a** out for karaoke. He can't sing!
2	I'm going to take	☐	**b** to martial arts.
3	Dad isn't cut	☐	**c** out when the art course begins.
4	Pete has really taken	☐	**d** up ballroom dancing!
5	Let's find	☐	**e** off in front of other people.

B Complete the text with these words.

> call out   called for   found out   show off   took to   took up

The Pavement Picasso

Ask anyone who has had the chance to see Julian Beever's art and they'll all say the same thing: You won't believe your eyes.

Julian has been doing his chalk drawings on pavements since the mid-1990s and he (**1**) _____ the form of art very quickly. These drawings create the illusion of being three-dimensional when they are viewed from the right angle. The technique (**2**) _____ is 'trompe l'oeil', which is a French technique he (**3**) _____ about when he (**4**) _____ the hobby. His work is so good that he has been called the 'Pavement Picasso'.

While Julian draws, the public often (**5**) _____ questions about his views on art, politics and life in general, and he loves talking to them, as he says his art is for the people. He believes art shouldn't be locked away in galleries and libraries, but should be free for all to see. So, not only is what he's doing entertaining, it's educational, too.

Julian had reason to (**6**) _____ this year. His art is so popular that a company published a book which featured a collection of photographs of his pavement art from all around the world.

Grammar

Modals & Semi-modals (2)

A Read the situations and write a sentence for each one using the correct modal form.

1 You definitely need to have a licence to fly a plane.

   _____

2 I'm thirsty. I'm going to ask you for some orange juice.

   _____

3 You don't need to buy bread. There's some in the kitchen.

   _____

4 It is necessary for you to leave the party at 11 o'clock.

   _____

5 There's no obligation for you to buy her a birthday present.

   _____

B Complete the text with these words.

can   have   to   must   needn't

The Empire run-up

Some people have very odd hobbies. In New York, USA, you can sometimes see people running up the stairs inside the Empire State Building! It's an annual race which you (1) _____ compete in only if you are invited.

The competitors have (2) _____ line up in the building's entrance and when the starting gun goes off, they (3) _____ to run up the stairs towards the top of one of the world's most famous buildings. The winner is the first person who reaches the finishing line in the Observation Deck, 1,576 steps later.

Even though the event can be dangerous, you (4) _____ have any special equipment. However, people say to minimise the risk of injury you (5) _____ train as much as possible beforehand.

Use your English

A Complete the text by writing one word in each gap.

The Moomba birdman rally

If you're interested in the idea of human flight, then why not go to visit Melbourne, Australia! Every year, the city celebrates *Moomba*, and it's the biggest festival in the country.

The most popular event at the festival is the Birdman Rally, (1) _____ is a unique flying competition. Some of the competitors are professionals in home-made high-tech machines, while others simply wear a pair of wings with feathers stuck on, or come dressed-up as a chicken! (2) _____ jump off a bridge and fly as far as they (3) _____ until they land in the river. Competitors (4) _____ to be over 18 years old and they (5) _____ be able to swim, of course. Apart from that, the activity calls (6) _____ creativity, imagination and a little bit of craziness! If people think they are (7) _____ to fly, the organisers want them to try!

To (8) _____ out more, look up *Moomba Birdman Rally* online and check out the videos on YouTube. They're incredibly funny!

Writing: a postcard

A Match the linking words and phrases 1–3 to their uses a–c.

1 for instance ☐

2 as well as ☐

3 because ☐

a to add information

b to give examples

c to say why something happens

Linking words and phrases

Remember to use linking words and phrases to make your writing flow better.

- Use *as well*, *too*, *and*, *also* and *as well as* to give extra information or to join similar ideas.
- Use *because*, *since* and *as* to explain why something happens.
- Use *for instance*, *for example*, *like* and *such as* for examples. You can't start a sentence with *such as* or *like*, but you can start a sentence with *for example* and *for instance*.

B Read the writing task below and then circle the correct words.

You are camping for the weekend with your school. Write a postcard to your family. In your postcard you should:

- *tell them about your holiday*
- *say what you are going to do tomorrow*
- *ask them about their weekend*

Write 35–45 words.

1 You will write a letter / a postcard.

2 It will be read by your school / your family.

3 You will / won't ask a question.

4 You will include information about tomorrow / next week.

C Read the example postcard and circle the best options.

Include a greeting.

Use informal language and different adjectives.

Include a question.

Hi Mum, Dad and Sally!

I'm having a great time at the campsite. The food is good. We had burgers (1) and / too salad last night.

We didn't go swimming yesterday (2) because / also it rained, but we are going today instead.

We've done some fantastic activities, (3) like / also hiking and mountain climbing. We've played football, (4) for example / too. Tomorrow we are playing tennis. What have you been doing? Miss you!

Bye!

Thomas

Include the plan for the next day.

Include an ending.

D Read and complete the *Exam Task* below. Don't forget to use the *Useful Expressions* on page 105 of your Student's Book.

Exam Task

You are on holiday with your grandparents. Write a postcard to your friend, Sarah, who is on holiday in New York. In your card you should:

- say where you are
- say what you have done
- say what you are going to do
- ask Sarah about New York

Write 35–45 words.

↻ Writing Reference p. 178 in Student's Book

Vocabulary

A Choose the correct answers.

1 I ___ lost while I was walking in the mountains. I was very scared.

   a did   **c** went

   b kept   **d** got

2 The unlucky explorers never reached their ___.

   a expedition   **c** congratulations

   b conditions   **d** destination

3 The runner could not ___ with the heat and had to give up his attempt to break the record.

   a get better   **c** panic

   b deal   **d** tolerate

4 The crew of the sailing boat ___ with terrible storms but managed to survive.

   a coped   **c** succeeded

   b destroyed   **d** disappeared

5 Edmund Hillary is one of the most famous ___.

   a companions   **c** explorers

   b destinations   **d** expeditions

6 The rescue team were amazed that the earthquake victims had ___ the extreme cold.

   a helped   **c** lived

   b died   **d** survived

7 We do our ___ to prevent accidents, but people participate in extreme sports at their own risk.

   a well   **c** help

   b best   **d** calm

8 If you want to get fit, why not ___ up martial arts?

   a call   **c** take

   b cut   **d** show

9 The man had been flying a balloon across the desert for five days when he went ___.

   a lost   **c** away

   b along   **d** missing

10 I love ___; I think the dancers are so graceful.

   a martial arts   **c** drama

   b gaming   **d** ballet

11 I am giving ___ judo because I get lots of injuries.

   a on   **c** with

   b up   **d** away

12 The temperature in the Arctic in winter can reach 30 degrees ___ freezing.

   a under   **c** until

   b down   **d** below

13 Climbing Mount Everest tests the ___ of your abilities. It's so difficult.

   a flow   **c** strengths

   b destination   **d** limit

14 Jim is a bit of a ___ off. He always boasts about how good he is at gaming.

   a show   **c** try

   b tell   **d** take

15 'Don't you just love taking pictures?'

'Yes, ___ is my favourite hobby.'

   a sculpture   **c** cookery

   b painting   **d** photography

16 Take this life jacket with you. It might just ___ your life!

   a take   **c** save

   b keep   **d** make

17 I love having ___ lessons at school. I want to be an actor when I'm older.

   a sculpture   **c** drama

   b painting   **d** ballet

18 Why don't you ___ for the football team at school? You're really good at sport.

   a find out   **c** cut out

   b try out   **d** call out

19 It's really hot today. It must be ___ 35 degrees Celsius!

   a over   **c** onto

   b along   **d** during

20 We finally reached the top ___ the mountain at five o'clock in the evening.

   a in   **c** of

   b over   **d** on

Grammar

B Choose the correct answers.

1 When the emergency services finally arrived, the survivors of the air crash ___ for days.
   a have been waiting
   b had been waiting
   c were waiting
   d are used to waiting

2 Neil Armstrong was the first astronaut to walk on the moon, where no man ___ ever walked before.
   a would   c could
   b has   d had

3 When the team reached the top, they ___ several members.
   a already lost   c had already been losing
   b had already lost d have already lost

4 'Who ___ the equipment for the expedition?'
   'It was John.'
   a did prepare   c prepare
   b prepared   d have prepared

5 'You won't meet Jane today.'
   'Why not? ___ invited her to the party?'
   a You didn't   c You
   b Haven't you   d Have you

6 '___ you enjoy hiking?'
   'No, I think it's very tiring.'
   a Does   c Didn't
   b Doesn't   d Don't

7 'Tom won the chess tournament!'
   'Really? Who ___?'
   a did he beat   c he beat
   b does he beat   d beat him

8 Let's go swimming with Jane and Tom on the river, ___?
   a do we   c will we
   b shall we   d won't we

9 You could teach me how to dance, ___ you?
   a could   c haven't
   b couldn't   d didn't

10 'Is that your sister jogging in the park?'
   'It ___ be her; she hates exercise.'
   a shouldn't   c can't
   b mustn't   d oughtn't

11 Sammy ___ be tired. She's been climbing all day!
   a need   c ought
   b can't   d must

12 Louise ___ take sculpture lessons, but it isn't certain.
   a can   c ought
   b may   d must

13 That was a great view from the top of the hill, ___?
   a isn't it   c doesn't it
   b hasn't it   d wasn't it

14 'I hurt my knee when I fell off my skateboard.'
   'You ___ to be more careful.'
   a ought   c might
   b must   d should

15 You ___ buy a new camera; you can borrow mine.
   a needn't   c shouldn't
   b mustn't   d couldn't

16 ___ you got anything better to do than watch TV all day?
   a Haven't   c Don't
   b Can't   d Needn't

17 You ___ go to bed early. It's Saturday tomorrow, so there's no school.
   a ought   c could
   b don't have to d may

18 He'll call me when he finishes, ___ he?
   a won't   c doesn't
   b will   d does

Reading

A Read the *Exam Reminder*. Are the questions in the same order as the information in the text?

_____

B Now complete the *Exam Task*.

The cost of high-tech teens

Exam Reminder

Finding the answers

- Remember to underline key words in the questions before you read the text.
- Write short notes about the topic of each paragraph as you read.
- Read the questions again and decide which paragraph the information is in. Remember that the questions are in the same order as the information in the text.
- Look for words and phrases in the text similar to the key information you underlined.

For Julie Westbrook, the final straw was the £280 her 15-year-old daughter, Ruby, spent on downloading music and horoscopes onto her mobile phone. For Simon Evans, it was a mobile phone bill totalling £370 for his teenage daughter's text messages. Both parents were absolutely furious that their children had run up such massive bills.

'When I was a teenager and wanted to be accepted by others, being cool meant wearing the right clothes and trainers and listening to the right music. You didn't need to spend a fortune to be cool,' says Julie. 'Nowadays though, teens seem to want to impress each other with their mobile phones, video games, computers and all sorts of other gadgets,' she adds.

These days, the cost of being cool has skyrocketed and one of the main expenses seems to be mobile phones. Teens want mobile phones in order to talk to and text their friends. Parents usually end up having to pay high mobile phone bills, with charges for hundreds of minutes of calls and thousands of text messages. And as if that wasn't bad enough, teens now want mobile phones with access to the Internet. Once they get them, they start purchasing applications, known as 'apps' for short, for their phones. What they don't realise is the high cost of this new technology.

'It's very expensive to have access to the World Wide Web from a mobile phone,' Julie says. 'That wasn't explained to me when I was choosing a mobile phone plan for my daughter. She downloaded four songs and those four songs cost me nearly £100. I was so upset that I cancelled the service as soon as the contract was finished.' But that wasn't the end of it for Julie.

'The next mobile phone company offered my daughter 200 minutes and unlimited texts for £19.99 a month, which seemed fair. I thought the problem had been solved, but then a bill came with another £80 in charges. Ruby had texted a code to get horoscopes sent to her and had been charged extra. I couldn't believe it!'

Julie says she hadn't realised what was involved in getting a mobile phone, or that it was going to be so complicated. She's

angry with the phone companies, too, for not explaining things clearly to her. 'Don't they understand that most parents have no clue about the technologies available for mobile phones?'

Simon Evans and his wife hit the roof when they got a £370 phone bill for their daughter's extra minutes and texts. 'Lydia had sent over 4,000 text messages and spent around 20 hours on her mobile in one month,' Simon says. 'If you do the maths, you'll see that's over 130 text messages and 40 minutes of talk time a day!'

Fortunately, Julie and Simon both found ways to control their teens' phone use. Julie eventually got a plan that allowed her to log in to an Internet account and check how much the phone was being used. Simon has limited how much his daughter can use the phone by getting her a card plan. When she runs out of minutes, that's it. She has to buy another card with her own pocket money.

'It's taught her the value of money,' says Simon. 'But she's also learnt something far more important – you don't need to have the latest high-tech gadgets to have value as a person.'

Exam Task

Look at the sentences below about the use of mobile phones. Read the text to decide if each sentence is correct or incorrect. Write **T** (True) or **F** (False).

1 Julie Westbrook's daughter spent a lot of money buying a new phone. ☐

2 Julie's daughter spent £280 on extra services for her phone. ☐

3 The writer thinks teenagers today don't care if they're cool or not. ☐

4 The writer thinks children should have the newest technology. ☐

5 Parents think their children know how to be responsible with money. ☐

6 Julie's main complaint is that she wasn't given enough information. ☐

7 Julie doesn't want her daughter to have a phone. ☐

8 In the end, Simon went online to check his daughter's phone use. ☐

9 Simon also makes his daughter pay for part of her phone use. ☐

10 Simon suggests that being trendy isn't the most important thing. ☐

Vocabulary

A Complete the sentences with these words.

> battery camera laptop microchip remote control research satnav USB stick

1 Can you pass me the _____? I want to watch a different TV programme.
2 If we had a _____, we'd know how to get to the party.
3 I put the files that I needed onto a _____ and took them home.
4 Our dog has got a _____ in case it ever gets lost.
5 I need to recharge the _____ on my phone.
6 My parents are buying me a new _____ so I can do my homework more easily.
7 _____ leads to the development of new technology.
8 He took hundreds of photos of the wedding with his new _____.

B Complete the text with these words.

> developed engineers experimented progress revolutionised

Archimedes' death ray

Ancient historians noted that in 212 BC when the Greek city of Syracuse, in Sicily, was attacked by the Romans, Archimedes devised a mirror that directed the sun's rays onto Roman warships and set them on fire. Archimedes, an ancient Greek scientist, had **(1)** _____ mathematics and physics, so many people believed that he was indeed clever enough to have **(2)** _____ such a death ray. Others disagreed.

The popular TV programme *MythBusters* tried to recreate Archimedes' death ray, but made no **(3)** _____ and decided it was impossible. However, a group of **(4)** _____ from MIT (Massachussets Institute of Technology) decided to try it themselves.

They built a model of part of a Roman warship and positioned it at the right distance. Then they **(5)** _____ with different shapes, formations and many different mirrors. They waited for a sunny day, and when it came, within minutes the warship was on fire! They had proved that the death ray was not a myth.

Grammar

The Passive Voice: Tenses; *by* and *with*

A Circle the correct words.

1 The results of the experiment will **be / been** presented tomorrow.
2 Yesterday, we were **tell / told** not to bring our mobile phones to school.
3 The new computer was installed **by / with** the new software yesterday.
4 The engineer was angry because he **wasn't informing / wasn't informed** of the changes to his design.
5 Many chemicals are used **by / with** scientists every day.
6 The school laboratory hasn't **being cleaned / been cleaned** since Monday.
7 The mobile phone was **buy / bought** in France last summer.
8 My computer was **repair / repaired** before I needed it for work.

B Complete the sentences with the correct passive form of these words.

> borrow develop fix not test send often use

1 Special equipment _____ in chemistry laboratories to do experiments.
2 Many books _____ from the library over the next year.
3 My computer _____ at the moment by the technician.
4 Our students _____ on biology in the exam next week.
5 The email _____ when the computer crashed.
6 The new product _____ by a group of scientists last month.

Listening

A Read the *Exam Reminder*. How many times will you hear the recording?

_____

B 🔊 9.1 ▶ Listen and complete the *Exam Task*.

Exam Reminder

Listening again

- Don't forget that you will hear the recording twice. Make a note of any answers you are unsure about the first time you listen.
- Check your answers and concentrate on the questions you haven't answered the second time you listen.
- Guess if you have to. Don't leave any answers blank.

Exam Task

You will hear an interview with someone who is talking about new technology. For each question, choose the correct answer **a**, **b** or **c**.

1 What is an e-reader?
  a a book which is installed onto a computer
  b a gadget which helps people to read paper books
  c a device on which electronic books are read

2 What does Ron say is the main advantage of an e-reader?
  a All the books that you download are free.
  b A lot of books can be stored on a light gadget.
  c It doesn't cost a lot of money to buy.

3 What is true of many e-readers?
  a They can store over 5,000 books.
  b You can read newspapers on them.
  c They help you read books faster.

4 How is an e-reader different from a traditional book?
  a The size of the letters can be changed.
  b You can't write in it.
  c It takes up more space.

5 In which situation would an e-reader not be beneficial?
  a on a trip
  b at college
  c in the garden

6 What does Ron say about borrowing an e-book?
  a It can be borrowed for a limited time.
  b It can be borrowed by many different people.
  c The person who borrows the book pays for it.

7 What is the main disadvantage of an e-reader?
  a It is hard to read.
  b It needs a battery.
  c It is easy to lose.

8 What's the interviewer's opinion of the e-reader in the end?
  a She thinks they're expensive.
  b She prefers normal books.
  c She's going to buy one.

C 🔊 9.1 ▶ Listen again and check your answers.

Vocabulary

A Circle the correct words.

1 Ask Ben how to use the satnav; he's an expert on / at them.
2 I was really concerned around / about my iPod after I dropped it, but it was fine.
3 We rely on / for technology a lot these days.
4 If I didn't have my mobile phone, I don't know how I would communicate to / with people!
5 The use of police helicopters leads in / to lots of criminals being arrested.
6 Environmentalists have been looking into / for answers to the problem of global warming for years.

B Complete the sentences with these words.

came communicate go instead rely successful

1 My dream is to visit Kenya and _____ on safari.
2 Centuries ago, Greek cities _____ under threat of attack by the Romans.
3 We have decided to buy a tablet _____ of a laptop because they are easier to carry.
4 Scientists have been _____ in proving that global warming is caused by people.
5 I can always _____ on my friends at school when I have a problem.
6 Do you believe that some people can _____ with animals and know what they are thinking?

Grammar

The Passive Voice: Gerunds, Infinitives & Modal Verbs

A Rewrite the sentences in the passive form.

1 Can they fix the problem? _____
2 You don't need to install it now. _____
3 I remember that you told me the answer. _____
4 She doesn't like it when people disagree with her. _____
5 You ought to tell him the truth. _____
6 I expect you to inform me. _____

B Complete the text by writing one word in each gap.

Computer hackers

Huge problems can be caused (**1**) _____ hackers and it has been shown that any computer system, even major government systems, can (**2**) _____ entered illegally. How does the hacker steal from the average person? First, details such as credit card numbers and bank account information have (**3**) _____ be found on people's personal computer systems. Then the details start to (**4**) _____ used to empty the money from your bank account. The best way to protect yourself from (**5**) _____ hacked is by not keeping sensitive information on your computer.

Use your English

A Complete the second sentences so that they have a similar meaning to the first sentences, using the words in bold. Use between two and five words.

1 We don't clean the computer screens every day.
   are
   The computer screens _____ every day.
2 Don't tell Tina what to do, she doesn't like it.
   being
   Tina _____ what to do.
3 I'm sure we can deliver the air conditioning unit tomorrow.
   be
   I'm sure the air conditioning unit _____ tomorrow.
4 We had to replace the old electrical system.
   to
   The old electrical system _____.
5 They asked the scientist to do the experiment.
   was
   The scientist _____ the experiment.
6 They have trained Amanda as a laboratory assistant.
   has
   Amanda _____ as a laboratory assistant.
7 They gave us bad news.
   we
   The news _____ was not good.
8 The students hadn't done the experiments carefully.
   done
   The experiments _____ carefully.

Writing: sentence transformation (2)

A Complete the words in these collocations.

1 t _ _ _ _ food
2 do j _ _ _
3 renewable e _ _ _ _ _
4 endangered s _ _ _ _ _ _
5 c _ _ _ with
6 fall in l _ _ _
7 p _ _ _ _ of
8 b _ _ _ _ up

B Read the writing task below and then decide if the statements are true (T) or false (F).

Here are some sentences about gadgets. For each question 1–5, complete the second sentence so that it means the same as the first. Use no more than three words.

1 The first sentence has the gap. ☐
2 The sentences are all about gadgets. ☐
3 You have to write three words in each gap. ☐

C Read the example task and follow the instructions.

> 1 Dan broke up with Amy in a text message!
>
> Amy _____ with by Dan in a text message!
>
> 2 New technology is being used to develop renewable energies.
>
> People _____ new technology to develop renewable energies.

1 Underline the collocations from A.
2 Circle the words in the first sentence that need to be changed to fit the second sentence.

D Read and complete the *Exam Task* below.

Exam Task

Here are some sentences about technology. For each question **1–5**, complete the second sentence so that it means the same as the first. **Use no more than three words.**

1 The Internet has been popular since the 1990s.
The Internet has been _____ many years.

2 I'm sure that's not the TV remote control.
That _____ be the TV remote control.

3 It isn't necessary for you to use satnav to find my house.
You _____ have to use satnav to find my house.

4 The robot is approximately the size of a four-year-old child.
The robot is _____ same size as a four-year-old child.

5 If you get a camera, you can come to the photography course with me.
_____ a camera, you can't come to the photography course with me.

Reading

A Read the *Exam Reminder*. Do similar words always mean the same thing?

_____

B Now complete the *Exam Task*.

1

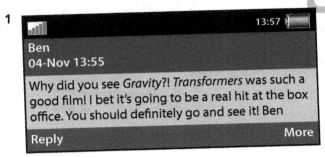

> **Ben**
> 04-Nov 13:55
> 13:57
>
> Why did you see *Gravity*?! *Transformers* was such a good film! I bet it's going to be a real hit at the box office. You should definitely go and see it! Ben
>
> Reply   More

2

> **Please make sure you bring your own sheet music to your audition.**
>
> Instruments will be provided, but you may bring your own if you prefer.

3

> Son,
>
> Please can you reschedule your drum lesson? We would like to collect you from school and take you shopping to enquire about some drum kits for you ...

4

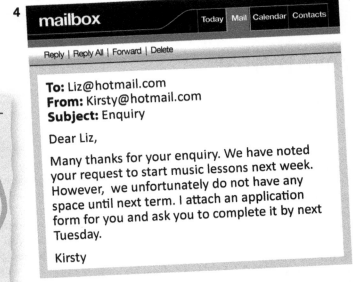

> **mailbox**   Today | Mail | Calendar | Contacts
>
> Reply | Reply All | Forward | Delete
>
> **To:** Liz@hotmail.com
> **From:** Kirsty@hotmail.com
> **Subject:** Enquiry
>
> Dear Liz,
>
> Many thanks for your enquiry. We have noted your request to start music lessons next week. However, we unfortunately do not have any space until next term. I attach an application form for you and ask you to complete it by next Tuesday.
>
> Kirsty

5

> **FOR SALE**
> **BAGPIPES**
> A couple of scratches
> Purchased 5 years ago
> Not suitable for under 5s
> Contact me on: 783 461

Exam Task

Look at each of the texts for each question. What do they say? Mark the correct letter **a**, **b** or **c**.

1 Which film did Ben see?
  a *Gravity*   **b** *Transformers*   **c** *Box office*

2 What must everyone take to the audition?
  a their sheet music
  b their own instrument
  c nothing, as everything will be provided

3 What do the boy's parents wish to do?
  a give him a drum lesson
  b take him to school
  c buy him a drum kit

4 The advert says the bagpipes are
  a in good condition.
  b not recommended for children below the age of 5.
  c less than 5 years old.

5 When does Kirsty tell Liz that she could start music lessons?
  a next term
  b next week
  c next Tuesday

Vocabulary

A **Complete the text with these words.**

> actors   director   documentary   lines   script   show

Big Brother

An advert on TV the other day said I should follow all of the 'action' on *Big Brother*. *Big Brother*? Isn't that the reality **(1)** _____ where people are in a house all day either sleeping or making coffee? Not much action there, really! But the oddest thing about programmes like *Big Brother* is that it isn't real. Sure, the 'stars' are ordinary people instead of professional **(2)** _____, but that's where the reality ends. The show can't be real if it's got a **(3)** _____ telling the participants what to do. Of course, this kind of show doesn't have a **(4)** _____ with **(5)** _____ for the participants to learn, but they know the viewers will vote them off the show if they don't give a good performance. They also know that most viewers want to see some kind of drama. Usually this leads to the participants behaving like idiots. Some viewers may like this, but it isn't my cup of tea at all. I prefer a good **(6)** _____!

B **The phrases in bold are incorrect. Write the correct ones.**

1 I think **soup operas** are really silly, but unfortunately, there are loads of them on TV.   _____
2 The actors were in the **clothing room** changing their costumes for the next scene.   _____
3 I love **real shows**, even though the action is controlled by the director.   _____
4 I'll meet you at the **boxing office** half an hour before the film starts, OK?   _____

Grammar

Reported Speech: Statements

A **Circle the correct words.**

I interviewed Jimmy Jackson about his very amusing hobby. He **(1)** told to me / told me he had a website for misheard lyrics where people **(2)** send / sent him the lyrics they thought they **(3)** hear / had heard in a song. When I spoke to him, Jimmy **(4)** said / told that mistakes could happen even with very simple lyrics. For example, he said that the lyric, 'With or without you' in the U2 song **(5)** was / is misheard by someone as 'We thought we found you'. One of his favourites, he **(6)** said / told me, was from the same song. The actual lyric is, 'Sleight of hand and twist of fate … ', but one person thought it was 'Slice of ham and piece of cake … '. Jimmy said that **(7)** his / my site was very popular. He also **(8)** informed / informs me that he would soon be bringing out a book of the funniest misheard lyrics.

B **Rewrite the sentences correctly.**

1 Jim told me I can borrow his CDs.   _____
2 Robert said that he had seen the film yesterday.   _____
3 Mr Hogg tells his students they would be putting on a play.   _____
4 I told Matilda that her book won't be published.   _____
5 Serena said she must get tickets for the opera.   _____

Listening

A Read the *Exam Reminder*. Should you write the same words that you hear?

_____

B 10.1 ▷ Listen and complete the *Exam Task*.

Exam Reminder

Completing information

- Remember to listen to and read the exam instructions carefully first.
- Then read the heading and the information. Think of words that would fit in each gap.
- Don't forget that you can write numbers as figures (*8*) or words (*eight*).
- Remember to write between one and three words and to write the exact words you hear.
- When you listen again, check your answers and spelling carefully.

Exam Task

You will hear some information about a concert by the Venezuelan Youth Orchestra. For each question, fill in the missing information in the numbered space.

The Venezuelan Youth Orchestra

The Venezuelan Youth Orchestra is celebrating its (**1**) _____ anniversary.

Age of the musicians: (**2**) _____

Famous reaction to one of their performances: (**3**) _____

Main aim of the Venezuelan Youth Orchestra: to make classical music a part of (**4**) _____

Place and time of the performance on Saturday: (**5**) _____ (**6**) _____

C 10.1 ▷ Listen again and check your answers.

Vocabulary

A Complete each sentence with one word.

1 Let's make sure we get tickets before they sell _____.

2 Miles told his father to turn _____ his awful old-fashioned music.

3 Someone in the street was giving _____ flyers about a concert.

4 The children acted _____ their favourite story, *Peter Pan*.

5 The security guard didn't like the way I was dressed, so he turned me _____!

6 Did you get those song lyrics _____ on paper last night?

7 I think Lady Gaga is too crazy to really catch _____ with everyone.

8 'I'm sure you'll grow out _____ hip-hop music,' Angela said to her teenage son.

B Match the first parts of the sentences 1–6 to the second parts a–f.

1 The new reality show hasn't really caught ☐
2 It turns ☐
3 She told me to turn ☐
4 Don't turn ☐
5 You should get the ☐
6 He was turned ☐

a website address down before you forget it.
b away from the concert because he wasn't old enough.
c off the TV. I'm watching this documentary.
d on, so it's going to be cancelled.
e up the radio because she loved that song.
f out that they eventually had six children.

Grammar

Reported Speech: Questions, Commands & Requests

A Make reported questions by writing the words in the correct order.

1 he asked / why / were following / the photographers / him / they _____
2 could / who / he / to the premiere / invite / Adam asked _____
3 the stage / me / was / where / she asked _____
4 borrow / he / Robbie / asked / whether / could / my camera _____
5 no one / why / clapped / Lucy asked / had _____
6 to the theatre / Matthew asked / get / me / could / how / he _____
7 whether / she asked / the film / had / seen / I _____
8 her / if / buy / Sheila asked / I / a ticket / could _____

B Change the direct speech into reported speech.

1 'How old is your sister?' she asked me.

_____

2 'Don't forget to feed the cat,' Mum told Mary.

_____

3 'Where are the batteries?' she asked Tim.

_____

4 'Stop watching that terrible soap opera!' Eliza told her sister.

_____

5 'Did you go to the concert last weekend?' he asked her.

_____

Use your English

A Choose the correct answers.

Lights! Camera! Action!

Which country has the largest film industry in the world? If you think it's the USA, you're wrong. The answer is, in fact, India. Nearly 3,000 films were (**1**) ___ in India in 2009.

The most popular films are action, comedy and romantic musicals. The musicals are beautiful productions full of colourful costumes and scenery with lots of people involved, including many dancers and singers. Imagine, one Indian film had 71 songs in it! That's a lot of (**2**) ___ to remember!

Film critics (**3**) ___ that most of these films tend to be predictable (**4**) ___ they have very similar stories, but it seems that the public don't mind at all! In fact, millions of people both in India and the rest of the world are huge fans, and tickets for new films sell (**5**) ___ quickly.

Indian cinema is often referred to as 'Bollywood', but it turns (**6**) ___ that the name is only correct for Hindi-language films; there are many other languages spoken in India. The name 'Bollywood' is a combination of 'Bombay' (the city now called Mumbai) and 'Hollywood', but 'Bollywood' isn't a real place. So if you're ever in India, don't try to find it!

1	a	produced	b	created	c	turned	d formed
2	a	lyrics	b	tracks	c	reviews	d copyright
3	a	tell	b	told	c	ask	d say
4	a	for	b	because	c	in order	d so that
5	a	out	b	in	c	out of	d down
6	a	up	b	away	c	off	d out

Writing: a letter or story

A Complete the sentences with these words.

after   finally   first   that   then   while

1 _____, we left the theatre and went home.

2 She was watching a soap opera _____ he was reading a newspaper.

3 _____ going to the ballet, they went to a restaurant.

4 First, the actor forgot her lines. After _____, she ran off the stage crying.

5 We are driving to the airport. _____ we are catching a plane to Mallorca.

6 _____ of all the actors met to practise for the play.

B Read the two writing tasks below and then circle the correct words or phrases.

1 *Your English teacher has asked you to write a story. Your story must begin with this sentence: Sarah stepped off the plane. This was going to be the best holiday ever!*

2 *This is part of a letter you receive from your cousin in America.*

At school I am writing an essay about schools all over the world. What do you do in a typical day at school? Please tell me so I can write about your school.

1 In question 1, you will write a letter / a story.

2 In question 2, you will write to your cousin / teacher.

3 In question 2, you will write about what happens at your school / give your opinion about your school.

Learning Reminder

Ordering ideas
- Remember that there are words and phrases to help you order your ideas when you write a letter or story.
- Introduce the first action with *First of all*, e.g. *First of all the actor came onto the stage.*
- For two actions happening at the same time, use *while*, e.g. *The audience listened while he performed.*
- For actions that happen one after another, use *then, after that, after* or *before*, e.g. *After he had finished, the curtain closed.*
- Introduce the last event with *Finally* or *In the end*, e.g. *Finally, the audience cheered and clapped.*

C Read the example letter and <u>underline</u> all the words and phrases for ordering ideas.

Hi Becky,

Thanks for your letter. Don't worry – I can definitely help you with your essay.

First of all we usually have a maths lesson. That starts at 9am. Then we study English before break. After break, we have a science class. Then we have lunch. After that we do art or drama. Finally, we study history or geography before going home at 3.30.

I hope this helps!

Love,

Nick

D Read and complete the *Exam Task* below. Don't forget to use the *Useful Expressions* on page 131 of your Student's Book.

Exam Task

Write an answer to one of the questions below. Write your answer in about 100 words.

1 This is part of a letter you receive from a pen-friend in Australia.

In school we are doing a project on what young people in Britain do on holiday. What do you usually do? Please tell me so I can write about you.

2 Your English teacher has asked you to write a story. Your story must begin with this sentence: *Tina was excited. This was her first trip to a rock music concert.*

▶ Writing Reference p. 177 & p. 179 in Student's Book

Vocabulary

A **Choose the correct answers.**

1 'The remote control doesn't work!'
  'I think you need to change the ___.'
  a USB stick   **c** satnav
  b batteries   **d** microchips

2 The singer said that these ___ were from his favourite song.
  a tests   **c** lyrics
  b lines   **d** scripts

3 If you read the ___, you'll find out how your new gadget works.
  a script   **c** remote control
  b lines   **d** instructions

4 The gadgets sold ___ within a few minutes of being on sale.
  a out   **c** on
  b off   **d** in

5 Hey Greg, turn ___ the music. I love this song!
  a off   **c** up
  b out   **d** down

6 Through the Internet, people can communicate ___ friends all over the world.
  a in   **c** from
  b to   **d** with

7 You can collect your tickets from the theatre ___.
  a dressing room   **c** soap opera
  b box office   **d** stage

8 'Why is this play so popular?'
  'Because it has a great ___, I suppose.'
  a lyric   **c** line
  b script   **d** stage

9 'I think my camera's broken!'
  'Give it to Jim. He's an expert ___ them.'
  a on   **c** at
  b from   **d** up

10 The teachers have put ___ a surveillance system in the school playground.
  a off   **c** out
  b in   **d** on

11 Some experts believe that books may come ___ threat from modern technology.
  a at   **c** below
  b under   **d** in

12 Students who want to be ___ should study hard at university.
  a success   **c** successful
  b successfully   **d** succeed

13 Tim dropped his mobile phone and it ___ to the bottom of the pool.
  a sank   **c** drowned
  b set   **d** turned

14 We're going ___ safari next year. I can't wait to see all the animals in their natural habitat.
  a in   **c** at
  b into   **d** on

15 Computers have ___ our work and leisure time.
  a installed   **c** revolutionised
  b experimented   **d** processed

16 'We have acted ___ the last scene hundreds of times.'
  'Then it will be perfect when the show opens.'
  a off   **c** in
  b on   **d** out

17 Can you give ___ one script to each actor, please?
  a down   **c** on
  b out   **d** off

18 The actors get ready in the ___.
  a stage   **c** box office
  b soap opera   **d** dressing room

Grammar

B **Choose the correct answers.**

1 My iPad should ___ later today.
   - **a** delivering
   - **c** be delivered
   - **b** to be delivered
   - **d** being delivered

2 There was a lot of excitement about a new gadget that ___ on the market.
   - **a** had put
   - **c** had been put
   - **b** has been put
   - **d** has put

3 The lights in this modern house can be turned ___ by remote control.
   - **a** away
   - **c** on
   - **b** out
   - **d** in

4 A message on my computer ___ me that I couldn't log in.
   - **a** said
   - **c** told
   - **b** asked
   - **d** sent

5 New batteries ___ for this gadget every few months.
   - **a** are needed
   - **c** are being needed
   - **b** are needing
   - **d** need

6 They looked for the USB stick, but it couldn't ___.
   - **a** found
   - **c** find
   - **b** be found
   - **d** is found

7 I don't understand why my computer ___ last night.
   - **a** was crashed
   - **c** is crashed
   - **b** crashed
   - **d** has crashed

8 My brother couldn't find the instructions and he asked me where ___.
   - **a** were they
   - **c** they are
   - **b** they were
   - **d** are they

9 Information about the school play ___ in class yesterday.
   - **a** gave out
   - **c** was giving out
   - **b** was given out
   - **d** had given out

10 My friend asked me why I ___ installed a satnav in my car.
   - **a** wasn't
   - **c** hadn't
   - **b** didn't
   - **d** couldn't

11 'Couldn't you get tickets for the show?'
   'No, they told us that all the tickets ___.'
   - **a** had sold out
   - **c** sold out
   - **b** did sell out
   - **d** were selling out

12 Before she borrowed it, Jane asked her brother how his camera ___.
   - **a** was working
   - **c** worked
   - **b** does work
   - **d** had worked

13 The pupils asked their teacher ___ a scene from the play to act out.
   - **a** recommending
   - **c** to recommend
   - **b** recommend
   - **d** could recommend

14 'Has Rick signed the contract for the show yet?'
   'He told me when we met last month that he'd signed it ___.'
   - **a** a week before
   - **c** a week ago
   - **b** before a week
   - **d** last week

15 Last year this sitcom ___ several prizes, including one for best new comedy.
   - **a** awarded
   - **c** were awarded
   - **b** was awarded
   - **d** was awarding

16 Can the robot ___?
   - **a** repair
   - **c** be repaired
   - **b** repaired
   - **d** repairing

17 She asked her sister ___ off the music.
   - **a** turn
   - **c** turns
   - **b** to turn
   - **d** has turned

18 My laptop ___ when I dropped it last week.
   - **a** damaged
   - **c** was damaged
   - **b** is damaged
   - **d** were damaged

Reading

A Read the *Exam Reminder*. What should you underline?

_____

B Now complete the *Exam Task*.

Where shall we visit this summer?

a Library of Congress

- America's oldest cultural institution
- Largest library in the world

Public tours for individuals and families:
Schedule: Monday–Friday, 7.30am, 11.30am, 1.30pm, 2.30pm, 3.30pm*

* no 3.30pm tour on Fridays; on public holidays the first tour is at 9.30am

For group tours:
Book in advance for school groups of 12 to 60 people
Schedule: Monday–Friday, 7am, 10am, 11am, 1pm
Closed to the public on Saturdays, Sundays, Thanksgiving Day, Christmas Day and New Year's Day

b National Museum of American History

- The greatest collection of American history
- More than three million items on display, including President Abraham Lincoln's top hat!

Open daily 10.00am to 5.30pm
Open 10.00am to 7.30pm on November 26, 27 and December 26, 27, 28, 29, 30
Closed December 25
Free admission, no tickets required
For groups of 20 or more get a discount at the *Stars and Stripes Café*.

c Washington Monument

The Washington Monument was built in honour of the first US president, General George Washington. It's the tallest stone structure in the world.
Open daily 9am–5pm
Summer hours: 9am–10pm
(May 31–September 6)
Closed July 4 and December 25
Admission is free but you must have a ticket.
Please note: Tickets run out quickly. To reserve tickets, go to http://www.recreation.gov, or call 1-877-444-6777 for individual tickets or 1-877-559-6777 for group reservations.

e National Air & Space Museum

- See the largest collection of historic aircraft and spacecraft in the world.
- Touch a rock sample from the moon!

Hours: 10.00am–6.30pm
Summer schedule: March 29–September 5, 10.00am–7.30pm
Open every day except December 25
Admission: Free
No parking is available at the museum.

f The United States Capitol

Take an official tour.
Allow enough time – there is a lot to see and do!
You must have a ticket.
9am–4pm, Monday to Saturday
Closed: Thanksgiving Day, Christmas Day, New Year's Day and Inauguration Day

d The White House

Visit the home of the President of the United States!

Tour schedule: 9.30am to 11.00am Tuesday to Thursday; 8.30am to 12 noon Fridays; 8.30am to 1.00pm Saturdays (except on public holidays)
Free of charge
Call the 24-hour line at 202-456-7041 for more information.

White House Visitor Center
- Open seven days a week from 8.30am until 4.00pm
- Interesting exhibitions
- 30-minute video

g The National Mall

An adventure for all ages, every step of the way
Full of history, culture, museums, beautiful sights and statues
Opening times vary.
Parking available

h International Spy Museum

Open 10am–6pm
Exciting interactive exhibitions and top-secret experiences
Recommended for adults and children over 10

Exam Task

The teenagers below are all looking for somewhere to visit on their school trip to the United States of America. There are descriptions of eight possible places to visit. Decide which place would be the most suitable for the following teenagers. For questions **1–5**, mark the correct letter **a–h**.

1 Victoria likes history but isn't very interested in the presidents. She wants to take her young 13-year-old cousin for the day and wants to be able to drive to the place. ☐

2 Lucy thinks the group will be hungry before or after visiting somewhere so she thinks it would be a good idea to get a discount to eat somewhere nearby. She really wants to see exhibitions and particularly something about an American president. ☐

3 Dan would like to go somewhere on Saturday morning, and would like to be able to find out more information at any time he likes in case he forgets to ask about something while he's there. ☐

4 Luke wants to go somewhere which opens until late in the afternoon. He hopes to see something from space. ☐

5 Sebastien wants to get up as early as possible during the week as there are so many places to visit. Which place should he visit first? ☐

Vocabulary

A Choose the correct answers.

education   exam   knowledge

1 A good _____ can help you have a great career.

applications   fees   grants

2 The _____ for the degree course are very high.

graduates   lecturers   tutors

3 It's hard for _____ to find jobs when they leave university.

university   primary   secondary

4 The first day at _____ school is often difficult for young children.

course   schedule   timetable

5 According to the _____, we have maths on Monday.

candidate   examiner   teacher

6 The _____ was sent out of the room for talking during the exam.

accent   pronunciation   sound

7 Roberto speaks English with an Italian _____.

lesson   studies   subject

8 My worst _____ is physics. I find it so difficult!

B Complete the words in the definitions.

1 A c _ _ _ _ _ _ _ _ is a person who is doing an exam.
2 The s _ _ _ _ _ _ _ are subjects like biology, physics and chemistry.
3 The a _ _ _ are subjects like drama, dance and music.
4 A f _ _ _ _ _ is what you keep your notes in.
5 A d _ _ _ _ _ _ is a document that shows you have passed an exam or finished a course.
6 A g _ _ _ _ is money you get to pay for your studies.
7 You do sport in a p _ _ _ _ _ _ _ education class.
8 A u _ _ _ _ _ _ is a set of the same clothes that all students at a school must wear.

Grammar

Causative

A Circle the correct words.

1 The school is have / is having the lab cleaned tomorrow.
2 Lucy had / has her school bag stolen last week.
3 Are they going to have the library paint / painted next week?
4 Mr Flynn has had / has his book published.
5 I had the application form sent / send to me by the college.
6 The college will having / will be having a swimming pool built next month.

B Complete the answers with the correct form of the verb *have*.

1 'Where's your car?' 'I _____ it repaired at the moment.'
2 'Is your computer OK now?' 'Yes, I _____ it fixed yesterday.'
3 'Where was Tom when I called?' 'He _____ his bike serviced.'
4 'Your hair is nice.' 'Thanks. I _____ it done every month.'
5 'Why weren't they at the meeting?' 'They _____ an alarm installed.'
6 'Where are the students?' 'They _____ their class photo taken.'
7 'Has Joe finished the report?' 'Yes, he _____ it sent by courier now.'
8 'What's wrong with the whiteboard?' 'I don't know. I _____ it checked later.'

Listening

A Read the *Exam Reminder*. What should you underline?

_____

B [11.1] ▶️ **Listen and complete the *Exam Task*.**

Exam Task

Look at the six sentences for this part. You will hear a conversation between two friends, a boy, Theo, and a girl, Maddy, about their school. Decide if each sentence is correct or incorrect. Write **T** (True) or **F** (False).

1 Theo enjoys Fridays at school. ☐
2 Theo practises playing the trumpet every morning. ☐
3 Theo thinks he will pass his maths exam. ☐
4 Maddy is studying *Julius Caesar* in her Performing Arts class. ☐
5 Theo has a rugby match on Wednesday. ☐
6 Maddy can choose which classes to go to on Friday afternoons. ☐

Exam Reminder

Thinking about the speakers

- Don't forget to read the instructions carefully first to understand what the listening will be about.
- Underline key words or phrases in the sentences. Then think about similar words that the speakers might use.
- Try to imagine what the speakers will say if the sentence is true and if it is false.

C [11.1] ▶️ **Listen again and check your answers.**

Vocabulary

A Circle the correct words.

1 You need to do / make an effort if you want to pass your exams.
2 If you smash / break the rules, you'll get in trouble.
3 Mark has got / found a taste for drama. He loves acting in plays.
4 How will you have / make progress if you don't do any revision?
5 He's not in / on his teacher's good books after failing his exams.
6 You'll soon get / take the hang of doing experiments in the lab.

B Complete the text with the correct prepositions.

Tilly goes to boarding school

Tilly was excited! Today was the day she started boarding school. Boarding school! Just like the characters in her favourite books. Ever since she had read the stories she had wanted to attend a school like that. She wasn't worried (1) _____ making new friends – she was good (2) _____ that and had never suffered (3) _____ being shy. Her parents had applied (4) _____ a place (5) _____ the best school in the country, and Tilly had been accepted. It was expensive, but her parents were happy to spend the money (6) _____ her education. They had visited the school and were satisfied (7) _____ the facilities. All Tilly had to do now was concentrate (8) _____ her studies and enjoy this new adventure!

Grammar

Gerunds; Infinitives; Gerund or Infinitive?

A Choose the correct answers.

| go   to go   going |

1 Do you want _____ to the library with me?

| help   to help   helping |

2 She can't _____ you with your essay this evening.

| do   to go   doing |

3 I don't mind _____ my homework straight after school.

| buy   to buy   buying |

4 It isn't worth _____ the most expensive computer.

| finish   to finish   finishing |

5 I'm too tired _____ this assignment tonight.

| study   to study   studying |

6 Grandma remembered _____ all night for her school exams.

| learn   to learn   learning |

7 They visited the museum _____ about ancient history.

| borrow   to borrow   borrowing |

8 Tim would rather _____ books than buy them.

B Find and circle the eight mistakes in the text below.

Time to study!

It was the night before the last exam. So far, Simon had done well, he thought. Of the six subjects he had studied in his final year of school, this last one – physics – was the most difficult. He wanted study medicine, so he had to get high marks in his exams being accepted into university.

Follow his physics teacher's advice, he had prepared for this exam by revise every day. 'You mustn't to leave it all until the last minute!' Mr New had warned. Simon cleared his desk, opened his folder and started look through his notes. They were neat, well organised and easy reading. After study for a few hours, Simon was ready for bed. That night, he dreamt of becoming a world–famous doctor.

Use your English

A Complete the second sentences so that they have a similar meaning to the first sentences, using the words in bold. Use between two and five words.

1 Someone is delivering the book to me tomorrow.

am

I _____ to me tomorrow.

2 'Yes, I'll help you with your project,' said Winston.

agreed

Winston _____ with my project.

3 The technician was fixing the computer when the electricity went off.

getting

We _____ when the electricity went off.

4 They painted the chemistry lab yesterday.

had

The school _____ yesterday.

5 It's bad for you to study all night.

not

_____ good for you.

writing: a report

A Complete the sentences with *both (of)*, *either (of)*, *neither (of)*, *or* or *nor*. Sometimes, more than one answer is possible.

1 Neither the students _____ the teacher knew the answer.

2 _____ classrooms have computers.

3 _____ the books can be used on this course.

4 These dictionaries are expensive, but _____ them are useful.

5 I want to study either science _____ medicine. I haven't decided yet.

6 We can spend our money on _____ a computer or a games console.

B Read the writing task below and then circle the correct answers.

You recently carried out a student survey on the school library as part of a social studies project. Write a report summarising two opinions mentioned in the survey and suggest how the library could be improved.

1 You questioned teachers / students.

2 Your report will focus on two opinions / all opinions.

3 You will make a complaint / suggestions for improvements.

C Read the example report and answer the questions.

State the reason for writing the report	**Introduction** This report will present the findings of a survey on the library at Lowbrough High School. It also makes recommendations for improvements to the library.
Discuss the first problem and make a suggestion for improvement.	**Books** Most students complained about the books in the library. They are either too old or in bad condition. Students think this prevents them from studying properly. It was suggested that the school buy more new books.
Discuss the second problem and make a suggestion for improvement.	**Study areas** Another complaint is about the study areas in the library. They are located by the windows, which are next to the playground. Consequently, it is often too noisy for students to study properly. The study areas could be moved to the back of the library, which is both quieter and larger.
Bring the report to an end by summing up the suggestions made.	**Conclusion** In conclusion, the main suggestions are to buy more books and to move the study areas to a better place.

1 What are students concerned about? _____ and _____

2 What are the solutions? _____ and _____

D Read and complete the *Exam Task* below. Don't forget to use the *Useful Expressions* on page 145 of your Student's Book.

Exam Task

You recently carried out a student survey on the school trips offered by your school as part of a social studies project. Write a **report** summarising opinions on two trips mentioned in the survey and suggest how these trips could be improved. (100–120 words)

12 The Body Beautiful

Reading

A Read the *Exam Reminder*. Does the correct answer option always use the same words as the text?

_____

B Now complete the *Exam Task*.

Exam Reminder

Choosing the best option
- Don't forget that if you see the same word in the text and in an answer option, it may not be the correct answer.
- Check it is the best option by reading the text with the same word carefully.
- Before you choose the best answer, read all the answer options.

Express yourself!

Tattooed man

A henna tattoo

Throughout history, humans have decorated their bodies in a variety of ways, by wearing jewellery, changing their hair or painting their nails, amongst other things. Humans have displayed a lot of imagination in their pursuit of beauty.

Some forms of decoration, however, can be quite extreme. And whether they make a person more attractive or not is usually down to an individual's taste. Take piercings and tattoos, for example. These forms of decoration are very popular nowadays. Those who are fans say that these are ways of expressing themselves rather than just decoration. And when you see how inventive and complex some tattoos are you might well agree. However, other people think that they are quite ugly, particularly big tattoos that cover large areas of the body or multiple piercings all over the head and face.

Whatever your personal opinion is, one thing is certain: unlike wearing make-up or changing your hair, piercings and tattoos can sometimes cause health problems. In order to understand how this can happen and what the dangers are, let's take a closer look at how they are done.

The most popular parts of the body for piercing are the ears, nose and belly button, although lots of people have their mouth or tongue pierced, too. Any doctor will tell you that piercing certain parts of the body can cause more problems than others. In the case of mouth and nose piercing, infection is a common problem because of the millions of bacteria that live in those areas. In addition, tongue piercings can damage teeth, while tongue, cheek and lip piercings can harm the gums.

Despite the pain and the health risks involved, more and more people are getting tattoos and this is possibly because so many celebrities have them. A tattoo is created by piercing the skin many times with a needle and injecting ink into the area. Tattoos are permanent because they are so deep. The top layer of your skin is the one that is produced throughout your life; this layer is always being replaced. But, it's the second, deeper layer of skin where the tattoo ink is injected. This layer of skin is not replaced, so the tattoo remains. The biggest health risk associated with tattoos is from viruses. Viruses from the needle can enter the body and cause serious problems.

And there's more trouble ahead. What happens if you get a tattoo and later decide that you don't really want it? You can have it removed by laser, but it's quite difficult and painful to remove a tattoo completely. Furthermore, while getting an average-sized tattoo takes a couple of hours, removing it can take several visits to the doctor, over a period of months. There's more bad news: tattoo removal isn't cheap and the procedure can cause infections and leave scars. Perhaps it is better to get a henna tattoo that gradually fades away after a week or two?

Are tattoos and piercings worth the risk? Be rational and ask yourself what's more important – health or fashion?

Exam Task

Read the text and questions below. For each question, choose the correct letter **a, b, c** or **d**.

1 What is the writer doing in the text?
- **a** persuading others to not follow celebrities
- **b** giving detailed information all about tattoos and piercings
- **c** giving advice on how to get a tattoo or piercing
- **d** describing why tattoos and piercings are so popular

2 What do some people believe about piercings and tattoos?
- **a** They show that you are popular with others.
- **b** They are complicated.
- **c** They are better than make-up.
- **d** They are a form of self-expression.

3 According to the article, what is true about tongue piercing?
- **a** Doctors say it doesn't cause any problems.
- **b** It makes you look strange.
- **c** It can damage the inside of the mouth.
- **d** It's the most popular type of piercing.

4 Why does the article suggest tattoos are so popular?
- **a** because they are safe
- **b** because they are permanent
- **c** because they are easy to remove
- **d** because famous people have them

5 What is the writer's attitude towards tattoos?
- **a** They are accepted by society.
- **b** They are not as important as good health.
- **c** They are necessary for some people.
- **d** They don't cause too many problems.

Vocabulary

A Complete the words in the sentences.

1 When you b _ _ _ _, you open and close your eyes quickly.
2 Air is pushed out of your nose very quickly when you s _ _ _ _ _.
3 You might c _ _ _ _ a lot when you have a cold.
4 When you are tired, you might y _ _ _.
5 If you're feeling bored, you might s _ _ _ a lot.
6 When you b _ _ _ _ _ _, air moves into and out of your body.
7 You b _ _ _ your food when you eat it.
8 If something is funny, you l _ _ _ _.

B Complete the text with these words.

| beard blood cheek chest eyebrows eyelid features neck |

A pirate from the Caribbean

Pirate Pete stood on the deck and looked out across the sea. He was sailing around the Caribbean in search of treasure. Around his
(1) _____ he wore a heavy gold medallion that rested on his
(2) _____. He had a long black (3) _____, dark bushy
(4) _____, and a scar on his left (5) _____, just under his eye, which he'd got during a sword fight. He also wore a patch over his right eye; his (6) _____ had been permanently damaged in the same fight many years ago. His (7) _____ were unusual, but he didn't mind. What he did mind was fighting. He hated it! In fact, the sight of (8) _____ made him feel sick, but sometimes a fight was unavoidable – he was, after all, a pirate.

Grammar

Adjectives; Adverbs; *so & such*

A Tick (✓) if the sentence is correct. Rewrite the incorrect sentences.

1 The celebrity wore a long purple beautiful dress. _____
2 Helen bought a pretty pink silk shirt. _____
3 Tom's got a little cute black and white bulldog. _____
4 I ate a delicious big chocolate chip cookie yesterday. _____
5 Let's get a comfortable big leather sofa. _____
6 The old man drove a red sporty Italian car. _____

B Circle the correct words.

1 Anna is so / such an intelligent girl.
2 I didn't find the magazine at all interested / interesting.
3 These fashion magazines are so / such silly!
4 The children were frightened / frightening by the loud noise.
5 It was so / such a lovely day that we went for a walk.
6 What a bored / boring film! Let's go home.
7 Maria has so / such beautiful skin, don't you think?
8 I felt exhausted / exhausting after the long walk home.

Listening

A Read the *Exam Reminder*. Why is it important to keep calm during an exam?

_____

B 🔊 **12.1** ▶❙❙ Listen and complete the *Exam Task*.

Exam Task

There are five questions in this part. For each question, there are three pictures and a short recording. Circle the correct answer **a**, **b** or **c**.

1 In the past, where did suntanned people often work?

2 What does this person find attractive?

3 What did the scientists show people pictures of?

Exam Reminder

Keeping calm

- Remember that being nervous during an exam will make it more difficult to understand the listening, so try to keep calm.
- Don't forget to underline key words in the questions before you listen.
- Look at the pictures and make notes as you listen. Write down any key information you hear.
- Don't worry if you can't answer all the questions the first time you listen. You will have time to read your notes and the questions again.

4 What small thing did Chinese people find beautiful?

5 What is the speaker's occupation?

C 🔊 **12.1** ▶❙❙ Listen again and check your answers.

Vocabulary

A Circle the correct phrasal verbs.

1 The tourists backed away / backed out of quietly when they saw the lion.
2 They got in the car and headed off / headed for the nearest hospital.
3 We've run over / run out of fruit juice. Can you get some from the shop?
4 Julie is always thinking over / thinking up excuses not to go to the gym.
5 Wearing bright red clothes will make you stand in / stand out in a crowd.
6 An employee of the gym was handing over / handing out leaflets in the street.

B Complete the sentences with these words.

> back   handed   head   run   stand   think

1 I finished the project last night and _____ it over to my teacher this morning.
2 Maria was so upset because her dog was _____ over at the weekend.
3 Oliver hurt his elbow, so Paul had to _____ in for him in the tennis match.
4 Would you tell me if you wanted to _____ out of the tournament?
5 We have to _____ off now because we're going to the salon soon.
6 You should _____ over what the doctor said about getting some exercise.

Grammar

Comparison of Adjectives & Adverbs

A Complete the sentences with these words.

> better   intelligent   quickly   saddest   tidier   worse

1 Why is your sister's room _____ than yours? Yours is a complete mess!
2 That was the _____ story I've ever heard; I can't stop crying!
3 Scientists say that this winter is going to be _____ than last winter, so make sure you have lots of warm clothes.
4 Henry runs more _____ than Dave. I think he'll win the race.
5 Joey isn't as _____ as his big brother.
6 I dance _____ than everyone in my ballet class.

B Complete the text with the correct form of the words in brackets.

Mind over matter

One of the (**1**) _____ (fascinate) and (**2**) _____ (certain) most difficult ideas to believe about human beings is that we may be able to influence our bodies and the world around us through the power of thought almost as (**3**) _____ (easy) as through our actions.

This idea is known as 'mind over matter'. Some scientists take the idea more (**4**) _____ (serious) than other scientists. The more they study the evidence, the (**5**) _____ (strong) their belief is that this amazing ability actually exists. They think it is one of the (**6**) _____ (important) discoveries about the mind in recent years.

Use your English

A Complete the text with the correct form of the words.

Fantasy vs reality

What is beauty? Is it in the faces you see on magazine covers? And why is it valued so (**1**) _____ in our society? Shouldn't we value (**2**) _____ far more than looks?

HIGH
PERSON

Our modern idea of what is (**3**) _____ is often the product of clever computer techniques which can (**4**) _____ change faces and bodies to make you look (**5**) _____, taller or generally more attractive than you actually are.

BEAUTY

EASY
THIN

But this isn't natural beauty. People come in all shapes, sizes and colours. The people we see in magazines are (**6**) _____ fake. And yet, the magazine editors claim that's what people want to see. They say people wouldn't be (**7**) _____ in buying a magazine with normal-looking models in it. But is that true?

TOTAL

INTEREST

Fortunately, we are slowly becoming aware that we should aim to be healthy, happy and (**8**) _____ with who we are. Young girls and women are particularly influenced by trends that can harm their health, but they need to realise that they are perfect just as they are.

CONFIDENCE

writing: a dramatic story

A **Match the first parts of the sentences 1–5 to the second parts a–e.**

1 It's possible to add suspense to a story ☐
2 A dramatic opening sentence will ☐
3 Using short dramatic sentences and direct speech will ☐
4 To help the reader imagine the characters and the action, ☐
5 Your writing will be more colourful ☐

a use descriptive adjectives and adverbs.
b by introducing a twist.
c give your story drama and variety.
d if it uses idiomatic expressions.
e encourage the reader to read on.

B **Read the writing task below and then decide if the statements are true (T) or false (F).**

Your teacher has asked you to write a story. Your story must begin with this sentence: Mike couldn't believe it.

1 You can begin your story any way you like. ☐
2 Mike was shocked. ☐
3 The story will explain why Mike felt that way. ☐

C **Read the example story and answer the questions.**

Set the scene and introduce the main characters.

Give background details about the characters' relationship.

Introduce a twist in the story and bring the story to an end.

Mike couldn't believe it. Did Greg really just slip a CD into his school bag? Mike stood there, amazed, while Greg whispered hurriedly to him, 'Quick! Let's get out of here!'

Mike and Greg were best friends. They met at high school and began hanging out together. They had a lot in common and enjoyed each other's company. When their friend invited them to her birthday party, they decided to buy her a CD by her favourite band. That's why they were at the Big Tunes music shop.

Now Greg was stealing. 'Are you for real? No way!' said Mike. 'Oh, come on,' said Greg, 'it's just a CD. They've got plenty more!' 'Take that CD out of your bag or I'll tell the shop assistant,' threatened Mike. Greg handed him the CD and ran out of the shop.

Mike knew his friend was disappointed with him, but he was sure he was doing the right thing. He also knew that their friendship was probably over.

1 Who are the main characters? _____
2 How do they know each other? _____
3 Where are they? _____
4 Something bad happens. What? _____
5 How does the story end? _____

D **Read and complete the *Exam Task* below. Don't forget to use the *Useful Expressions* on page 157 of your Student's Book.**

Exam Task

Your teacher has asked you to write a **story**. Your story must begin with this sentence: *Jenny felt let down.* (100 words)

↻ Writing Reference p. 179 in Student's Book

Learning Reminder

Making stories more interesting

You can make your stories interesting in several ways.

- A dramatic opening sentence will make the reader want to continue reading.
- Using descriptive adjectives and adverbs will help the reader to imagine the characters and the action.
- Remember to make your writing more colourful by using idiomatic expressions.
- Add variety and drama by using direct speech and short dramatic sentences.
- To add suspense, introduce a twist to the story in which something unexpected happens.
- Remember to include an interesting ending to the story.

Vocabulary

A **Choose the correct answers.**

1 'Learning a new skill is always hard at first.'
   'Yes, but we'll soon get the ___ of it.'
   a taste   c good
   b hang   d length

2 'How is your daughter doing at school?'
   'Her teachers say that she's making good ___.'
   a effort   c progress
   b books   d journey

3 'Why are you in such a bad mood?'
   'I'm worried ___ the test today.'
   a from   c for
   b about   d with

4 With her strong personality and beautiful features, Sally really ___ in a crowd.
   a stands out   c stands in
   b backs away   d heads for

5 ___ for the exam are asked to hand in their application form by the end of the week.
   a Graduates   c Examiners
   b Certificates   d Candidates

6 'Have you hurt your arm?'
   'Yes, when I bend it I get a pain in my ___.'
   a ankle   c calf
   b hip   d elbow

7 Dad's French ___ is so terrible that no one in France can understand him.
   a lesson   c diploma
   b certificate   d accent

8 'Can you think up a story for our project?'
   'No, I've ___ ideas.'
   a dropped out of c backed out of
   b run out of   d stood in for

9 The ___ is very strict. He never gives anyone high marks in the exams.
   a examiner   c tutor
   b graduate   d lecturer

10 What future is there for someone who leaves secondary school without any ___?
   a exam   c courses
   b qualifications d information

11 The treatment was such a ___ that the doctors expect him to recover soon.
   a success   c successfully
   b succeed   d successful

12 If you've got a cold, please remember to use a handkerchief when you ___.
   a yawn   c blink
   b sigh   d sneeze

13 Be careful when you cross the road. You don't want to get ___ over.
   a stand   c head
   b back   d run

14 The chemistry ___ is so hard that many students drop out before the end.
   a education   c subject
   b course   d knowledge

15 He tried to pass the music exam four times, but each time he ___.
   a passed   c lost
   b failed   d missed

16 As soon as the bell rang, the pupils ___ the door.
   a headed for   c ran over
   b headed off   d handed out

17 If I were as good ___ painting as Dean, I'd study art.
   a on   c for
   b at   d with

18 I was terrible at acting at first, but I'm getting the ___ of it now.
   a hang   c progress
   b taste   d best

Grammar

B Choose the correct answers.

1 Our lecturer expects ___ our projects to her before Thursday.

  a us handing in   **c** to hand in

  b us to hand in   **d** handing in

2 'Look! It's our old primary school teacher!'

  'Yes, I'm trying ___ her name.'

  a remembering   **c** to remember

  b remember   **d** to remembering

3 'Aren't you playing tennis any more?'

  'No, I've stopped ___ because I hurt my ankle.'

  a to play   **c** play

  b played   **d** playing

4 'What's wrong with your computer?'

  'I've got to ___ because it's not working at the moment.'

  a have it repaired **c** be it repaired

  b have repaired it **d** had it repaired

5 John was ___ tired that he fell asleep during the exam.

  a such   **c** as

  b so   **d** very

6 This is ___ a popular course that students are advised to sign up early.

  a very   **c** often

  b so   **d** such

7 'I don't remember what time the exam starts.'

  'How could you forget ___ important information?'

  a such   **c** so

  b such an   **d** as

8 When Mum was at school, she wore a(n) ___ uniform.

  a ugly grey school

  b grey ugly school

  c school grey ugly

  d ugly school grey

9 John writes ___ that he's always the last person to leave the classroom.

  a so slow   **c** too slowly

  b slowly enough   **d** so slowly

10 After a few weeks in bed with a broken leg, Dad was not ___ fit as he usually is.

  a the   **c** than

  b as   **d** very

11 Clare can't run ___ as her brother, who has very long legs.

  a quicker   **c** more quick

  b as quickly   **d** as quick

12 'Joe really takes after his father.'

  'Yes, he has the same personality. He's certainly ___ his dad.'

  a as funny as   **c** not as funny

  b as funny   **d** funny as

13 Chris was ___ pupil in the class and he got a grant to attend a top university.

  a more intelligent

  b a most intelligent

  c the most intelligent

  d the more intelligent

14 The human brain can do many creative jobs ___ a computer.

  a more well than **c** as good as

  b better than   **d** as best as

15 'Don't you remember meeting me before?'

  'I'm sorry, my memory is getting ___ as I get older.'

  a worst   **c** as bad

  b more bad   **d** worse

16 Julie has got such ___ hair.

  a long blonde lovely

  b blonde long lovely

  c lovely long blonde

  d lovely blonde long

17 I would like ___ why you haven't finished your homework!

  a knowing   **c** know

  b to know   **d** knew

18 You'd better ___ to your teacher for being late.

  a apologising   **c** apologise

  b to apologise   **d** apolgised

Notes

Notes

Notes

Notes

Notes

Notes

Notes

Notes

Notes

Notes

Notes